Kristy Chambers was born in Adelaide, South Australia, in 1975. After graduating from university as a nurse at age thirty, she worked in several hospitals around Australia and wrote this memoir. It is her first book, if you don't count the novel she wrote in her mid-twenties and eventually shredded, which was no great loss for the literary world, only the trees.

She currently lives in Brisbane, intends to run away to New York City for a while and is uncomfortable speaking about herself in the third person because it's weird.

KRISTY CHAMBERS

Get Well Soon!

(UN)
My Brilliant Career
as a Nurse

First published 2012 by University of Queensland Press
PO Box 6042, St Lucia, Queensland 4067 Australia

www.uqp.com.au
uqp@uqp.uq.edu.au

Cataloguing-in-Publication entry is available from the
National Library of Australia
http://catalogue.nla.gov.au/

ISBN 978 0 7022 3920 5 (pbk)
ISBN 978 0 7022 4823 8 (ePDF)
ISBN 978 0 7022 4824 5 (ePub)
ISBN 978 0 7022 4825 2 (kindle)

Typeset in 11.5/16 pt Bembo by Post Pre-press Group, Brisbane
Printed in Australia by McPherson's Printing Group

The author has changed the names of the characters in this memoir, and
some characters are composites of a number of people. This has been
done to protect their privacy. The truth of the story remains.

University of Queensland Press uses papers that are natural, renewable
and recyclable products made from wood grown in sustainable forests.
The logging and manufacturing processes conform to the environmental
regulations of the country of origin.

For my Mum and Dad, who are the best.

Contents

In the Beginning   1
Anorexiaville   7
Crazytown   17
Maxfax   27
Thahn   32
Zoe   44
Sheila   53
Shit   61
Sarah   67
Dennis   76
Christos   84
The Ancient Miner   93
Genevieve   99
Princess   109
The Tampon   118
Leo   125
Albert   133
Callum   141

Chris P Bacon   149
Pass the Parcel   157
Louis & Jeanette   166
Bill   181
Jacinta   189
Rochelle   197
Shane   205
Don   214
Things I Do Not Understand   222

Epilogue   231
Acknowledgements   235

In the Beginning

I first tried nursing on for size when I was 15 and went to the Goulburn Valley Base Hospital for two weeks of work experience. Everybody said nursing was a good idea – my parents, my teachers and the school careers advisor, *none of whom were nurses.*

'It's a great job!' they chorused. 'You'll never be unemployed! You can help people *and* see the world!'

I had my tonsils removed when I was seven and, as far as I knew, nurses were just the nice people who brought you ice-cream and jelly in hospital. What I *thought* was a nurse was actually a waitress, so when I said I'd give nursing a shot, I was in for a rude shock.

On my first work-experience day at the hospital there was ice-cream and jelly, just as I remembered. But there was also skin that looked and smelled like a rotten potato, adults wearing nappies, ulcers, pus, missing limbs and fingers, green plastic bowls full of poo, phlegm and vomit, tracheotomies and people crying. I wanted out. Nursing was *shithouse.*

I made it through the first week.

'Maybe you'd like to be a midwife? Work with babies?' one of the nurses suggested at the start of my second week.

'Yeah, maybe,' I agreed. Babies are cute and smell better than old people. So I went to the maternity ward for a day and they showed me a video of a woman giving birth. Her water broke, splashing all over the floor. Then she was down on all fours, mewing and moaning like a wounded animal while a baby's head came out of her, and I thought I might vomit. Now, not only did I not want to be a midwife or any other kind of nurse, I also no longer wanted to be female.

On my last day, the nurses asked me if I was going to be 'one of them', and I thought about it for half a second.

'Um, no offence,' I said, 'but there is no way on earth I would be a nurse . . . I wouldn't mind being a doctor, though. Nobody tells them what to do.'

They all laughed, and said that was fair enough, and I felt a bit sorry for them. I was 15, and sure I was destined for bigger and better things.

Apparently not.

The question that a lot of people like to ask is: 'How long have you been a nurse?'

Depending on the day, and how I'm feeling, I might just say, 'A couple of years now,' or I'll vent, 'A few years but it feels much, *much* longer.'

The next question is usually, 'And do you enjoy nursing?' and the response, again, hinges on my mood.

'Oh, it's pretty good, I guess,' I might say, or, 'I like the bit where I go on holidays.' Or, 'Right now I'm trying to figure out what else I can do with my life so I don't end up throwing myself in front of a train.'

And even when I badmouth the hell out of nursing, most people empathise and nod their heads, saying, 'Well, I could never do your job, *that's* for sure!'

'What do you do?' I ask, and they say things like, 'Oh, I'm an accountant,' or, 'I work in IT,' or, 'I'm a beautician and I wax people's swimsuit areas all day long.'

And I think, *Shit, your job sounds awful, nursing's not that bad.*

But some days, it really is.

I never had a strong inkling where a career was concerned. I only knew what I liked, and that there was no such thing as a job being a globe-travelling, booze-swilling, notebook-scribbling bourgeois pig, so I was screwed. I was going to have to marry well or work for a living, and since I didn't have a boyfriend, the wedding option seemed pretty unlikely. Employment beckoned, and I resented it greatly. I was *born* resentful.

I wandered around, lost, for a decade. An early attempt to study Creative Arts was hampered by my intolerance for the rampant wankery wrapped around it, so I spent some quality time on the dole, then worked a bunch of jobs I neither liked nor cared about before finally running away to London. After a couple of years spent in English pubs, as both an employee and a lush, I returned home just as spectacularly unqualified and work-shy as ever, but my most notable work-related achievement was now the time I headbutted Jude Law in the chest when I tripped in a Soho street on my way to pick up coffee for my boss.

My family collected me from the airport, and before we had even left the car park I wanted them to turn the car around; Australia seemed sleepy and boring and dry and brown. I was going to have to dig my way out of the hole I was in, as I had used up my allotted working visa, and because my grandparents had selfishly decided to be born in Australia instead of in Scotland like *their* parents had been, I was stuck. My future looked like a giant, gaping chasm of nothingness and I could barely stomach the thought of another shit job, so I was going to have to study *something*.

I narrowed it down to nursing or teaching, jobs with good prospects for overseas employment and which seemed meaningful enough not to drive me to despair. And while the thought of going back to 'school' at 26 filled me with dread, the fear of being trapped in menial-job purgatory forever was far greater. I took a cue from my younger brother, who was in the first year of his nursing degree and liked it well enough, put in a last-minute application and crossed my fingers. In retrospect, my brother may not have been the most fitting example for me to follow. He worked part-time in a nursing home and *liked* it, while I worked in a nursing home *once* and cried, then went home and drank a bottle of wine to try to forget about it. Still, the decision was made, and a few months later I found out that I had been accepted. I was going to be a *motherfucking nurse*. The 15-year-old me shook her head in disgust and called me a dildo, but she hadn't yet spent a year working in a supermarket and hating it with a passion, so I paid her no mind.

Having a sense of purpose was refreshing for me, and for my parents, and, for the first few months of study at least, I was excited. I went to all my lectures and tutorials and even though I felt very old, I also felt very superior to all the school leavers who didn't know shit about shit, and youthful in comparison to some of the other mature-age students, who looked older than the automobile. Actually using my brain, and using it for good instead of evil, was probably the best part of university for me, but before long my limited attention span crashed, and the novelty of education began to tarnish.

By the end of my first academically lacklustre year, I felt increasingly uneasy and worried that I had barked up the wrong tree by choosing nursing, because I could already tell I didn't much like where it was leading. I had just finished my first two-week placement in an oncology ward, time primarily spent showering old people and helping them off the toilet, and I hadn't loved it. *At all.* I thought about switching to a degree in education, now that I had a full year of study under my belt, because I quite liked the *idea* of being an English teacher and talking about books and writing and teaching kids how to spell. But I was all too aware that teenagers were arseholes, since I had been one myself, and that I would probably scream myself hoarse just trying to get anyone to listen to me, let alone learn anything. The positive of teaching was that I would get three months' holiday each year and I wouldn't have to see old people naked or deal, literally, with other people's shit. The negative was that I would have to be a teacher. So it became a matter of deciding who I *least* wanted to spend time with: teenagers or sick people.

As you can see, nursing was hardly my 'calling' in life, like it is for some people. Florence Nightingale didn't appear to me in a vision, and angels didn't fart into my ear at night, telling me to tend to the sick and diseased. I just decided that sick people trumped teenagers. Admittedly, that was well before I knew what 'melena' was and long before 'The Tampon', or else I would be a teacher right now.

Anorexiaville

In the second year of my degree, we began to drift away from the university campus and roam out into the nursing wilderness. The first year had been heavily theory based, with just two weeks in hospital, but the second year had a higher quota of practical placements, and mine began with a month in mental health. When I reported at seven am for my fortnight at the eating disorders clinic, everyone was lined up for the pre-breakfast Monday morning weigh-in. The girls were pretty, skeletal overachievers, giving me the side-eye and probably correctly calculating my Body Mass Index on sight. It was confronting in a lot of ways. I felt like a lard-arse in the company of some of the world's skinniest girls, and I was ashamed of myself for even making the comparison. They were super-thin because they were super-sick and I was healthy, not fat, but my own dieting ghosts were stirring.

'Jumper off please, Kate,' one of the nurses, Jenny, said in a bored tone to a girl further back in the line.

'But I'm *freezing*!' Kate whined, hugging herself and

stamping her feet like she was stuck outside in a snowstorm instead of a centrally heated, carpeted corridor in a private hospital. She had a white feeding tube stuck up one nostril, fixed in position across her cheek with a strip of white tape, and you could see the bones in her face.

'*Kate!*' the nurse snapped, and Kate gave her a filthy look before she lifted the heavy woollen jumper over her head and threw it on the floor. A couple of the other girls sniggered.

'Well, if I get pneumonia and *die* it's going to be *your fault*!' Kate said bitterly.

'You're not getting out of weigh-in, Kate, so cut it out.'

Kate simmered down. When she finally stepped on the scale and it showed she had lost 0.74 kilograms – despite the night feeding and the therapy and all the drugs – she smiled at the nurse in a smug, self-satisfied way, like she had won something.

Maybe the first girl who starved herself to death got a trophy, or a sash.

The anorexics didn't have much time for the bulimics. Although there was a high degree of behavioural overlap, people generally seemed to pick a tribe and stick with it, like on *Survivor*.

'Bulimics are anorexics who need to try harder,' I heard one of the reed-thin girls say. She was pushing a metal stand around the ward, a bottle of milky liquid hanging upside down from it, the contents of which were slowly flowing down her naso-gastric tube. She was doing laps, trying to burn off the kilojoules before they could accumulate anywhere in her body. Her pyjama pants billowed out around her bony, bird-like legs.

My stomach rumbled. I had woken up late and hadn't had time for breakfast before running out of the house, which seemed an oversight in fairly poor taste considering my surroundings. I went on my morning tea-break early, and had a piece of toast and a cup of shitty instant coffee, and actually paid attention to the act of eating for a change. Eating was a reflex; something I did when my body asked for it, usually insistently and loudly until I complied, or automatically commanded in the presence of cake. Constantly overpowering such a primal urge seemed a superhuman feat, and I could understand how doing so made somebody feel powerful and in control. And even though throwing up was definitely not my idea of a good time, the bulimics at least got to have a bit of fun first, eating anything and everything before they did whatever ugly, cut-throat shit was necessary to get rid of it. I thought I would choose their tribe, if pressed.

It was an all-girl crew on the ward when I was there, and these girls were cranky and emotionally volatile, but starvation does that to a person, I guess. For the most part, they smoked like Chinese factories, drank coffee, cried, then used up any small amount of energy exercising, running off the food they were forced to eat and trying to avoid the people who were pissing them off, which was everybody, because they were so irritable, because they were starving. Such was the cycle of life in Anorexiaville. It seemed an utterly miserable place to live, and was depressing enough just to pass through as a detour on the way to the third year of my degree.

As a student you were usually assigned a 'preceptor', a nurse who, in theory, took you under their wing and guided you through the duration of your clinical placement. Sometimes you were welcomed with open arms by an enthusiastic mentor who was keen to pass on their skills and knowledge, and sometimes you were barely tolerated, adding to the workload as your undergraduate presence invariably did. Actions that would normally be performed in autopilot nurse mode had to be explained in tedious step-by-step detail, but at least there was another set of (somewhat clueless) hands to assist with the basic chores.

On my first day I trailed a couple of different nurses, getting an overview of the clinic's daily operations, helped make a few beds and did a lot of reading from thick medical encyclopaedias. I went home and paid more attention to the act of preparing and eating dinner than I had in years and realised that I *loved* food. The good, the bad, the takeaway, I loved it all.

On the second day I did the morning observations, measuring blood pressure with tiny cuffs meant for children, and locating weak pulses nestled beside jutting bones. Mid morning, a blood-curdling scream came from one of the rooms. A timid, red-headed girl with a history of horrific, lifelong sexual abuse, and resultant post-traumatic stress disorder, was curled up in a ball in the corner, rocking back and forth and crying her eyes out. Someone had taken a shit in her bed, a shocking surprise that completely capsized an already keeling emotional state. It was assumed that a psychiatric patient from the acute part of the hospital had wandered up to the unit and randomly chosen her bed as a toilet, but nobody knew for sure, and it didn't matter now, the damage was done. She was distraught and hysterical.

The nurses consoled her and I went to the linen room to get some new sheets for her bed. It was depressing not being able to do anything to really help, but what could anyone say or do to make it better? And I don't just mean the shit, I mean *all* of it.

You could take her grandfather out the back and shoot him for molesting her since she was born, I suppose – that seemed as good a place to start as any.

Spending time at the clinic was beneficial for me. From a career point of view, I knew I didn't have it in me to work in a place like that five days a week, so it was yet another area to add to my nursing exclusion list, but it also made me grateful for my health. I have had major issues with food in my lifetime, most acutely as a teenager, and most events and times in my life are automatically recalled in the context of my dress size or weight at the time, with almost Swiss precision, a dysfunctional blueprint set in my youth.

I was a chubby ten-year-old, a dieting 13-year-old and a very thin 16-year-old, even subsisting on green apples and black coffee for a time, but I never possessed the steely determination anorexia nervosa demands. My work ethic was, and still is, appalling, and anorexia was a full-time, thankless job, one with long days and restless nights, a very high rate of burnout, and a 10–20% chance of death. But I was not as far removed from the girls in the clinic as I would have liked to think, either. I still bullshitted myself that a diet would work and that happiness would set in when a magic number was shown on a set of bathroom scales. So I had some of the same hang-ups, perhaps, but luckily, I fell far short of the extreme examples before me. It was not inevitable that I would have early onset osteoporosis, or be rendered infertile. The hair on my head wasn't dull and falling out in clumps and the corners of my mouth didn't split painfully if I tried to smile. I didn't have hard calluses on the backs of my hands from shoving them down my throat 50 times a day, from throwing up *water*, and I didn't want to disappear. These girls were winning at losing, dying right in front of your eyes.

Of the many horrors I was exposed to within the walls of the Eating Disorder Unit, 'Group Time' was the worst for me, personally. It may not have been in the same life-threatening category as dangerously low sodium levels from abusing box after box of laxatives, or as unsettling and disturbing as a stranger defecating in your bed, but if it were possible to die from embarrassment, it was going to happen attending a group. And those suckers were compulsory, especially for a second-year nursing student, so the real nurses could go on a long coffee break and have some peace and quiet. I didn't begrudge them their personal space, until I actually went to a group, and from that point on I begrudged the shit out of them.

Alyssa was a brand-new psychologist, fresh off the boat from university, and she was in charge of most of the groups. She couldn't have been more than 22 and was perky as hell. I was 28, a full-time student and already jaded. We didn't have much in common. I didn't know what to expect when I was forced to attend Alyssa's first group, but I hoped I wouldn't have to do any gross 'getting to know you'-type activities. I followed all the girls into the room, and saw a box of kitchen items tipped over on the floor. There were empty jars, containers, saucepan lids and wooden spoons in a big pile. My heart sank.

'Okay, everyone! Grab an "instrument"!' Alyssa said gaily, putting instrument in air quotes with her fingers.

The girls did as they were told without any obvious enthusiasm, and sat down in the circle of chairs with their selected ice-cream bucket, pair of serving spoons or colander.

'You look like a drummer, Kirsty!' Alyssa said, misreading my laminated student ID, and handing me a Tupperware container and a wooden spoon. I cringed all over. I wasn't eight years old, and I wouldn't have been less embarrassed if I were. Alyssa seemed to think that bashing cutlery on an upturned bucket for five minutes was going to be cathartic. For someone raped daily from five years of age, like at least one of the girls in the room, I very much doubted it. It was rage *making*, not resolving. I was already 100% angrier than I had been before entering the room.

'Okay, everyone! I call this "music therapy"!' she said. 'Let's really think about how we're feeling, channel that negative energy out, and make some *noise*!'

The only noise I wanted to hear was the fire alarm going off, so I could get the fuck out of there. All the girls were wearing their poker faces. They did as they were asked, mindlessly tapping away at their 'instruments', but it was the accompanying blankness, the absence of anything like resistance, that was most disturbing to me. The session made me want to peel out of my skin, and everybody else was completely blunted. Except for that dipshit, Alyssa, who was shaking two jars of rice like they were maracas and grinning.

I often saw one of the patients, Lucy, heading out of the grounds as I was arriving at the clinic. She was going out for her morning run, and she had an afternoon run and an evening run, too. She had that grotesque lollipop look happening: her head seemed over-large compared with her twiggy arms, legs and neck.

Lucy was on her fifth admission to hospital, and each time she got a little better but not enough to stay away for good. She was friendly but guarded, and always asked me questions about my studies and who I lived with, and if I had a part-time job or a boyfriend. It felt like she was try-ing to find out what life looked like outside the one she was having. We talked about travelling, among other things, and I mentioned that I really wanted to visit Japan.

'I want to go there, too,' she said.

'You should!' I told her, and she gave me a dry smile.

'Yeah, maybe,' she said, and implicit was the addendum *but I won't*. A trip to Japan wasn't for her, because nothing was for her. She wouldn't let it be. Her self-imposed restrictions extended well beyond food.

Lucy was beautiful, even with the skin stretched taut across her cheekbones and a pallid, sickly complexion, and she was much smarter than me. She had been dux of her high school and had the grades to get into medicine, but had had to defer when her weight loss really accelerated and she wound up in hospital. Now she wanted to be a dietitian, to turn an obsession into a career. She was at least halfway there already, a dedicated amateur, and knew more about metabolic and physiological processes than I ever would.

Lucy kept to herself and was a model patient in a lot of ways, going to all the groups and doing everything she was supposed to, but she scared me the most. The other patients might cry or scream, but Lucy was completely locked down, self-contained, like she'd been embalmed.

Anorexia has one of the highest mortality rates of any mental illness, and it's not just because of the physical wasting away, but also because self-harm has been turned into a barely resisted routine, the norm. The overwhelming leap to death by suicide has been reduced to a mere step by the time you weigh 32 kilograms and your most primal instinct – to live – has been subtly worn away like soap.

Get Well Soon!

I left the clinic on my last day, glad to be done and certain that I wouldn't be returning. The first half of my mental health placement was over, and next up was two weeks in Crazytown, an adult acute mental health ward at a huge public hospital. In the meantime, there were two whole days of pizza and beer in store and while it may not have been nutritionally optimal, it tasted great.

Crazytown

I was diagnosed with depression at 15 and come from a family with a very long, rich history of mental illness. The 'crazy' is strong with my people, so I don't use the word with any kind of malice or unkind intention. There is just no other word to cheerfully describe the chaotic atmosphere of an acute mental health ward. 'Batshitfuckingcrazytown' would be more apt, at times, but sounds much less friendly.

I turned up to the psychiatric ward for my next two-week placement, not knowing what to expect and wondering if somebody would try to stab me with a pair of scissors or a pen, or if any of the patients would be like Jack Nicholson in *One Flew Over the Cuckoo's Nest*.

Nothing that dramatic happened. I just found myself cornered all day long by chatty Cathys who had the incredible ability to tell stories that went on and on and *on*, and at the same time went absolutely nowhere. They would follow me around the ward like sheepdogs, separating me from my preceptor and the rest of the nurse herd so they could get some one-on-one attention and bore my brains out. The days felt extremely long and the only part I really looked forward to was lunch.

I did acquire some useful skills and insight, though. I learnt how to make people think I was listening when they were speaking to me when I was, in fact, not listening at all. And I learnt that, like the other nursing flavours I had sampled to date, Acute Mental Health was not my favourite either.

On the first day I was greeted by singing. Not good singing, or even average singing, but loud and most definitely persistent. The woman wouldn't *stop*. It was the same song, the same lines, over and over. Everybody seemed to be doing their best to ignore it, to just tune it out, but it was an uphill battle. Naomi, the nurse I was paired up with, had a hard time orientating me to the day-to-day running of the ward with her train of thought being constantly derailed by:

'Amazing grace, how sweet the sound!

'Amazing grace, how sweet the sound!

'Amazing grace . . .'

'How long has she been doing this?' the new doctor asked, frowning. It was his first day on the ward too, and he was struggling to concentrate, trying to write up medication for another patient whose blood pressure had gone through the roof.

'A week,' Naomi said.

He looked up sharply. 'No way!'

Yes way. No wonder the nurses all looked exhausted,

like they wanted to drop to the ground and cry. It's the little things. They become rather enormous after a while.

I made a new friend named Greg on that first day. He was 45, had a crooked fringe that he cut with craft scissors, teeth brown from smoking and drinking 12 cups of coffee a day and wildly crossed eyes. Even if he weren't on a psychiatric ward, you would totally pick him out of a line-up as someone with strong mental anomalies. He had been here for two weeks this time around, with ongoing delusions. He asked me if I could pick something up for him when I finished for the day and handed me a drawing of a badge that he wanted to have made. It said, *Prime Minister of Australia*. People's delusions are so fancy, they're always Jesus or Buddha or someone like that, never some pockmarked, divorced dude who works in a shoe store and wants to do a tandem skydive on his 40th birthday.

Maybe it was because he thought he was the prime minister and felt a responsibility to take charge, but Greg had assumed the role of unofficial ward caretaker. He had recently rugby tackled a patient who had tried to throw a chair through a window, and it made him feel good. So good that he started looking for trouble so he could fix it, and there was an increasing risk that he was going to start *making* trouble, like starting a fire, to get his fill of 'justice'.

I was sitting at the nurses' station, a clerical island in the centre of the ward full of desks and chairs and the patient charts, when Greg started yelling. He was gripping another patient, a plump woman called Gwen, by the elbow and hollering from the doorway of the television room.

'Help her! Somebody help!'

Gwen had a personality disorder and a slight brain injury, and she was holding both hands over her crotch like she was trying not to piss herself, but there was already a spreading wet patch on her grubby tracksuit pants. She started jumping from side to side, and came right up to the desk where I was. I subtly rolled my chair back a little.

'Alright, Gwen, calm down,' one of the real nurses said, gathering a bunch of paper towel to soak up the spill.

'I'm pregnant!' she wailed at me. 'My waters broke!'

Gwen looked a little long in the tooth to be gestating, but you just have to roll with it.

'Really . . . how many weeks are you?' the nurse asked.

'Fifty!' she shouted.

'*Oh, no!* My waters broke *again!*' she exclaimed and started hopping around the room, still holding on to her crotch for dear life.

'*Somebody do something! It's an emergency!*' Greg screamed hysterically, shadowing Gwen like he was spotting a weightlifter at the gym. One of the other nurses steered Gwen to the shower and another tried to talk Greg down from the top of his panic mountain. The receptionist called the cleaner and asked him to come and mop the floor before somebody slipped and broke their neck and there was a *proper* emergency. When people fall over in hospital, it is a total pain in the arse. There are a million bullshit forms you have to fill out, and nobody wants to deal with that amount of paperwork. Plus there really isn't enough space on the forms to write, *[your name here] sustained injury when slipped in pool of urine of delusional, mildly psychotic patient with phantom pregnancy.*

After a few days of following Naomi around, I was assigned two patients to look after, under her close supervision. Jodie was patient number one and, before I was even introduced to her, she announced that she had 'had enough'. I thought she meant that she was suicidal, but she didn't. She had been on the ward for a while, and had been trading 'favours' for drugs. Nothing illicit, she said, just other people's medication, but she had reached the end of her rope.

'That's it!' she said, angrily. 'I'm not sucking him off *anymore*! And he keeps getting this scabby thing on his dick, and today I said, naaah, that's *it*! He can keep his medication, I don't wannit! I'm not touching that scabby thing again. It's *gross*!'

'You haven't done it before, when it's scabby, have you?' Naomi asked, after a momentary pause.

'Oh yeah, heaps of times, but *that's it*! I'm not sucking him off ANY! MORE!'

'Well, good for you,' Naomi told her, and then, without missing a beat: 'Jodie, this is Kristy. She's a nursing student and she's going to be looking after you today.'

I smiled weakly.

Tennille was patient number two. Our introduction was positively low-key, compared with meeting Jodie, and she seemed an appropriate level of mentally ill for a second-year student brain. I felt much less intimidated.

Towards the end of the shift, Tennille walked up to the

desk where I was writing my notes and said disgustedly, 'Oh, *great*, that whistling sound is back again!'

'What whistling sound?' I asked her.

'Can't you *hear it*? It's that high-pitched whistling sound! I can't believe you can't hear it! There must be something wrong with your ears!' She was incredulous and impatient. Clearly, I was just not right in the head.

I cocked my head like a dog, listened, but got nothing other than the usual ward noise.

'No, I really can't hear anything–' I told her.

'Oh, you've got to be *kidding me!*' Tennille said scornfully, then gave me a filthy look and stomped off to her room.

It was entirely possible that something was wrong with my ears, I have seen a lot of loud bands in my lifetime, but it was equally possible that the noise was just static in Tennille's head. Since her alleged alien abduction and all the testing they did, the unusual had seemed to trail her like a shadow. We were tuned to very different frequencies, which I was glad about, but it made for a difficult, rather prickly rapport. She gave me the shifty side-eye for the rest of my prac.

My final casual acquaintance on the ward, Neil, was gently crackers; a lank-haired gentleman with thick Buddy Holly glasses and a cane and the slow-motion, shuffling walk of a proper psych patient. He had schizophrenia, and had established 'cog status' in the large machine of government payments and services that controlled his life. He was a hospital 'frequent flyer' and wore a bumbag clipped around his waist at all times, even when he was asleep in bed. It contained all his essential items: meds, smokes, keys, cash, cards with various mental health appointment dates and times, Centrelink's phone number and his case manager's contact details. He was ready for almost anything.

Neil loved a chat, and enjoyed sharing his thoughts on various topics to whoever happened to be nearby, which in this instance was me. He leant against the counter, hovering over me while I compulsively read another patient chart. I couldn't help myself, they were as addictive as crack, a mixture of David Lynch-calibre weirdness, heart-shattering sadness and accidental comedy that often made me laugh out loud, and left me looking like a rather unsympathetic arsehole, which I pretty much was.

'Alcohol is a very strong drug, and a legal one, too,' Neil said randomly, shaking his head.

'Yep, it sure is,' I agreed, sticking a pen in the chart so I wouldn't lose my place.

'Yes.' He collected his thoughts, then continued on a new arc: 'I have a lady friend, she stays at my house but she sleeps in the lounge and I sleep in the double bed. No kissing or touching or shaking hands or anything . . . I want to stay sex free and emotionally undisturbed.'

'Oh . . . right.' I wasn't sure where this conversation was going, but it felt like a gross over-share was just around the corner.

'No, no sex for me, that's for sure! She's a bedbug, though! That's what I call her, Bedbug!'

The tea lady rescued me from further personal disclosure

about Neil's sex life, or lack thereof. It was afternoon tea-time. Thank god.

'Coffee! That's another drug! And *it's* legal!' Neil called out over his shoulder as he ambled off to get a cup.

I nodded and smiled. It's all that can be done sometimes.

The next day, Neil was in a right flap at the nurses' station.

'I've got a problem! A big problem! My lady friend is at my house and she's *locked in and she's not answering the phone*!'

'What?'

'I need to call the police! Maybe she's ransacked the house and taken e-everything I own! Maybe she's in t-t-trouble!' Neil was winding up, beginning to stammer and visibly tremble. We told him to slow down and begin his story at the beginning, instead of the middle where it was currently idling.

Neil had been to see his doctor a few days previously, and the doctor had sent him directly to hospital, so Neil's lady friend, whom he had locked in the house, was *still* locked in the house, and he was going to be in hospital for at least another week. So he had called her from the hospital to let her know where he was and when he would be home. She hadn't answered and naturally Neil assumed the worst.

'There could have been a *fire*! Oh no! I've *killed her*!' he blurted, totally freaking out.

Everyone tried to reassure him that things were fine, but Neil could not be placated. He called the police and asked them to go and see if his house was still standing, because he was sure it was nothing but a smouldering pile of ash now, and that his Bedbug had been cremated.

The police phoned the ward back an hour or two later, wanting to speak to Neil, who had been lightly sedated by then. They had called around to his house, and his lady friend had opened the front door and talked to them, although admittedly through the locked screen door that only Neil had a key for.

'Can anyone say "deprivation of liberty"?' one of the nurses muttered.

Bedbug was fine, the police reported. She had enough food and toilet paper, would answer the phone from now on and climb out of a window if there was any kind of emergency. The house was very much intact, which was a huge relief to Neil.

'Oh, *thank you*, officer! That is a load off my mind! I was so worried, because I'm very unwell in hospital, you see . . .' He chewed the ear off the poor cop on the phone for a few dizzy minutes, then phoned home.

Apparently his lady friend had found a novel way to entertain herself. She was getting stoned on Neil's psych meds, eating Zyprexa tablets in front of the idiot box. With his arson fear now extinguished, and strangely unfazed by the possibility of Bedbug overdosing, Neil completely relaxed, and became as calm as a pond. It was everybody else who was uneasy, still unsure if his lady friend was actually a house guest or a hostage.

★

My preceptor, Naomi, filled out my assessment paperwork on my last afternoon and asked how I had liked my two weeks. I told her the ward was definitely an interesting place to visit, but I wouldn't want to live there. She nodded her head thoughtfully, and was about to say something when one of the patients suddenly began screaming at the top of her lungs, just screaming without pausing, by the front door. Naomi looked over at the wailing woman, then back at me.

'Where's your next placement?' she asked.

'Um, I've got two weeks in Maxillofacial Surgery and Ear, Nose and Throat next,' I said.

'Oh, okay,' she replied, nodding, as the screamer stopped and took a deep breath, preparing to unleash the next tier of her inner demons. 'Let me know if it's any good, I've got to get out of here.'

Maxfax

My next stint at the hospital was in 'Maxfax', as the Max-illofacial Unit was colloquially known. I thought it was the saddest place in the hospital, which was a big call in a giant glue factory where people dropped like flies every day. Dying was sad, but waking up and *wishing* you were dead was sadder still.

Maxfax was the home of patients whose faces had been disfigured by a pub glassing or a car accident, or ravaged by a malignant tumour or some other kind of trauma or disease. It was the ward you came to if you couldn't be patched up in Emergency, if you had fallen over and prac-tically sliced the nose off your face, for instance. It was the last stop before you were whisked off to the operating theatre for the first in a long string of reconstructive sur-geries. The patient was prepped and the doctors hoped that the skin graft they had harvested from another part of the patient's body would remain viable, so they could have the basics in life, like a nose and a mouth. Because beauty was not on the inside, no matter what your mother, or anybody else, told you. It was right there on the outside, where everybody could see it.

Like every other prac, I was assigned to a nurse buddy, who I clung to like a barnacle throughout my two-week stint. I had tried to choose wards that seemed somewhat interesting, and didn't sound as gross to me as Gynaecology or Colorectal Medicine did. Since Maxfax was from the neck up, I figured the patients would probably be more independent and self-caring, which meant less toileting, showering and exposure to other people's body wastes and, therefore, would be less disgusting. I was wrong.

The Ear, Nose and Throat patients shared the same ward with the Maxfax patients, so there were a lot of people with tracheostomies, which is where a hole is cut in your throat and a tube is inserted to assist breathing. 'Trachies' could be temporary or permanent, and bypassed the need to breathe through the mouth and nose, which might not be possible because of a tumour, or some other airway obstruction.

I walked into the first four-bed bay to say hello to the patients I'd be looking after during my shift. One man with cancer had just undergone a total laryngectomy, which meant his voice box had been removed, and he could now only breathe through the permanent opening in his neck. He tried to say hello to me, which made him cough, and he instinctively covered his mouth as a plug of yellow mucous shot out of the plastic tube in his throat and landed on the sheet in front of him like a rotten oyster.

His embarrassment, as he blushed wildly and fumbled for a tissue, killed me. He mouthed 'Sorry' repeatedly, wheezing noisily through his tube. I smiled and told him not to worry about it, trying to make light of the situation, but it was not a good start to the day. He was mortified, I felt like crying and it wasn't even time for morning tea.

The patient in the single room across the corridor, William, had just returned from radiation therapy. He had his back to me when I knocked on the door to introduce myself and when he turned around I tried to act casual and unperturbed, but it was shocking to see his face. There was a hole where his nose should have been, and a bulging flap of skin that had been cultivated from a thigh graft covering the left side of his face. The skin flap was like a big chunk of clay that would eventually be shaped to recreate his lost nose, as long as it stayed alive, so we had to continually monitor it for blood flow and make sure it stayed rosy and pink. Any discolouration was a bad sign, a warning of imminent soft tissue death.

I asked him how he was feeling after the radiation. He said he was a little nauseous, so my nurse buddy supervised me as I pretended to be a real nurse and gave William antinausea medication and checked his pulse, temperature and blood pressure. He sat on the edge of the bed, watching television with his back to the open door and the passing pedestrian traffic in the corridor. He must have been so sick of people staring at him with startled, horrified expressions and then looking away as quickly as they could, like disfigurement was catching.

It was a fairly quiet shift and most of my patients were having an afternoon nap, so I sat with William in his room and we watched *Entertainment Tonight* because the television was broken and only one channel worked. The irony of watching a program so vapid and superficial and consumed with 'beautiful people' in this ward, of all places, was faintly amusing and kind of sickening, too.

'This is the worst show on television,' I said. 'I can feel my brain shrinking.'

He smiled crookedly. 'Yeah, it's a shame the cricket's not on.'

I was on his right side. In profile, William looked like any other middle-aged man, just a little more tired and weathered with a dark shadow under his eye. After a while I didn't really notice his face, but when I saw the before and after photos in his chart that showed the rapid progression over 12 months from a slightly reddened area on the left cheekbone to an all-consuming football-sized tumour, the difference was jarring. The photos explained everything: William's slumped shoulders; the anti-depressants and anti-anxiety medications; the towels hanging over both the mirrors in his room. And all because a bunch of stupid cells wouldn't stop multiplying and dividing.

Maxfax was a bummer, on the whole, but I liked the patients, *and* there was a really good-looking doctor, which probably didn't make people like William feel so hot, but it worked out pretty well for me. Not only was he attractive in the face, but this doctor was also sympathetic to students and went out of his way to explain things to me, like inflammation and infection. I'm not sure exactly, because I was distracted by his looks and not really listening, but at one point he earnestly explained that if a particular patient lifted his arms above his head, he would turn red and automatically stop breathing.

This struck me as funny.

'Really? Wow! I might get him to try it this afternoon for a laugh,' I said, and the doctor looked appalled. So I had to tell him that it was a joke, and by then it didn't even seem funny to me anymore. I guess it never would have worked out between us.

Thahn

Study was the shit sandwich in the picnic of my life. I was forever poor, so instead of relaxing during the university holidays, which admittedly were generously long and seemed to come about rather quickly, I looked for extra work to supplement the income from my weekend bar job. And I complained about it *the whole time*. I wanted the money, but I also wanted it to turn up without my having to lift a finger. Not only did I *expect* something for nothing, but I cracked the shits when it didn't eventuate. I've learnt to accept that's just the sort of unreasonable brat that I am.

I was a dreamer, not a worker. When I was six years old, the teacher handed out sheets of paper that had a monkey in the top left-hand corner, and a bunch of bananas in the lower right-hand corner, with a maze separating them. The teacher told us to draw a line to get the monkey to the bananas. Instead of going *through* the maze, I drew a line around the outside of it, a large L, straight down and then across the page. There didn't seem much point going into the maze and getting all disorientated and lost when you could just go around the side. The teacher saw what I had done, and told me it was wrong. I was confused. I had got the monkey where it was supposed to go, in the easiest fashion possible. I hadn't had to do much work, and neither had my little monkey friend, and that's the way I liked it, an easy life with a minimal amount of effort. Twenty-two years later, nothing had changed.

One of my heinous extra jobs was at a call centre. I didn't last long there, but it sure felt like forever. The only thing I liked about it was the junk-food vending machine in the staffroom and pretending I was Madonna when I put my headset on. The novelty wore off quickly, though, when I had to stop using the headset as a theatrical prop and actually start calling the people on the computer screen in front of me.

'Come on, people! We've got a big target to reach today! *Let's go!*' The boss had a paunch, a shit haircut and a large Adam's apple. He clapped his hands together and tried to drum up enthusiasm among his hostages, all of us held prisoner by the promise of a dollar. I thought hateful thoughts and sighed unhappily.

We began dialling our way down a long list of allo-cated numbers, under fluorescent strip lights that made everybody's skin look grey and waxy. It was a fundraising campaign for a university, cold-calling the alumni to hit them up for cash. Most of them had long since graduated and didn't seem to feel at all indebted to the institution that had been the venue of their tertiary education.

'Good evening, my name is Kristy and I'm calling on behalf of the University of–' I only got as far as the beige opener when the curt 'Not interested!' hit my ear. Only 499 to go then.

The alumni list wasn't at all selective. Anyone who had ever set foot on the campus got a phone call, and most of them, unsurprisingly, were less than thrilled to hear from me.

'What *is it* with you people? I'm sick of you calling from India and trying to sell me things! You're like Jehovah's Witnesses, except over the phone!'

One irate caller was incredulous when I told him I was calling to raise money for the university.

'So, let me get this straight. You're asking *me* for money, because of what the university has done for me?'

'Uh, yes. I guess,' I said, reluctantly. Dude was hostile.

'I only graduated last year! I haven't even got a job! You should be giving *me* money! I've got a HECS debt for 30 grand, and I'm on the fucking *dole*! So what has that piece-of-shit university done for me, exactly?'

The boss tapped me on the shoulder and mimicked cutting his throat, so I just hung up. He could listen in on your calls without you knowing, and did, to make sure you were being friendly and polite and not swearing back at any of the rude callers.

I looked around at the other phone jockeys. Most of them were broke students like me, but planted among us like spies was a gang of professional telemarketers who brushed the abundant rejection off like lint and persuasively powered their way to 'target'. They stood out because they were enthusiastic. I wondered what the collective noun for them would be. A nuisance of telemarketers seemed most appropriate. And a murder would work too.

Two bays across from me was a girl in a motorised wheelchair. She had no arms and tiny stumps for legs and her own special headset, which was fancier than ours. It had an extra arm with a little rubber pad on the end and her head moved from side to side as she used it to type on the keyboard. They should have been sending her door-to-door if they wanted to raise some money, because she was wasted in a non-visual medium. People would have been falling over themselves to give a donation. She saw me looking at her, smiled and rolled her eyes, and I smiled and rolled my eyes back at her. She obviously hated this job, too, and it was probably one of her few options for employment. So, it wasn't enough that she was limbless, but she had to work in telemarketing as well. Goddamn it, life could be cruel.

Somebody made target and the boss let out an obnoxious holler: 'Let's hear it for Jodie, everyone! First person to make target tonight! Let's give her a round of applause!'

There was a smattering of weak claps from around the room.

'*Let's goooooo, team!*' he yelled.

Okay, that's it, I thought. *This is hell.*

The next crappy job was at a suburban coffee shop I renamed Bitch Café, where I spent my day making soy lattes and chai on skim milk for dismissive menopausal hags who spoke to you as though you had been lobotomised.

The only good thing about these lousy jobs was that they made nursing seem a whole lot more appealing, which was no mean feat given my inherent apathy. As the holidays wound down, I was practically champing at the bit to get back to studying. The sooner I went back to university, the sooner I graduated, and the sooner I could get a real job, and never have to do this soul-destroying bullshit again.

One of the few perks of being a second-year nursing student, besides ready access to Band-Aids, was that with one year of the degree under your belt, you were eligible to apply for work as an Assistant In Nursing (AIN), which was the polite term for a general shit-kicker. I signed up with an agency to do some casual shifts. My bar job was no great shakes, but it offered reliable, permanent hours while agency work was notoriously haphazard. Some weeks you might be offered six shifts in a row, and then none at all for the next two months.

You weren't allowed to do very much as an AIN, because you were still an untrained chimpanzee compared to a *real* nurse, but if a hospital required a glorified babysitter for a fairly straightforward, uncomplicated patient, then an AIN could plug the hole, freeing up the competent staff for proper medical work. AIN shifts were basically *paid* on-the-job training, while wearing a nylon polo shirt with the name of the nursing agency embroidered on the front, and yet another ugly laminate on a lanyard round your neck that screamed out your ASSISTANT IN NURSING status in block letters. The agency wanted everyone to know that you were a gimp, and not an actual nurse, so that you weren't asked to do more than you were capable of. And as a second-year nursing student, what you were capable of doing was pretty much squat.

My first ever shift as a shiny new Assistant In Nursing was at a private hospital, and my mission for the afternoon was to supervise a 90-year-old lady who was agitated, which sounded like a piece of piss. Evelyn wasn't demented, but she was becoming increasingly irritable and restless. The doctors weren't exactly sure what was going on, but because she was 90, and her bones were just *begging* for the chance to break, she was given around-the-clock monitoring to make sure she didn't end up on the floor, or die without someone noticing for an embarrassingly long period of time.

I introduced myself to ancient, wrinkled, white-haired Evelyn, who was rocking gently back and forth in bed. She gave me a cursory glance when I spoke to her, said nothing, and continued rocking.

'Do you need to go to the toilet or anything, Evelyn? Do you want me to help you up to the bathroom?' I asked her. I thought I'd hit the ground running, but Evelyn shook her head.

'Well, let me know if you need anything,' I told her, although she gave me no indication she was listening. She continued to rock, I read a book and the first two hours of our time together passed very pleasantly, in peaceful, mutual ignorance.

At five o'clock it was time for dinner, and I spoon-fed Evelyn some mashed vegetables. She smacked her lips together noisily but refused to eat more than a few mouthfuls. There was a cup of coffee on her dinner tray, though, and she definitely wanted that, so I helped her to drink it, and unsurprisingly, her agitation increased.

'Coffee . . . drink . . . more coffee,' was all she said, repeatedly, for half an hour. I rang the buzzer and asked one of the completely registered nurses what I should do.

'Just give her more coffee, if that's what she wants,' the nurse said, as blasé as could be. I was uneasy. It sounded like shitty advice to me. The first cup hadn't done her any favours, and I didn't think more of the same was a smart move, but what did I know? I was just the hired help, so I did as I was told. I gave Evelyn another cup of coffee. And then she *flipped the fuck out*.

I formulated a theory that caffeine was the missing ingredient in Evelyn's original recipe for Crazy Old Lady, and I think I was on to something because an hour after the second cup of coffee, Evelyn was screaming the place down.

'Coffee! Drink! *More coffee!*' soon progressed to 'HELP ME! GET AWAY FROM ME! I AM IN AGONY!' and left me looking like an elder abuser. Her wailing brought the nurses running, and the same one who had suggested I 'just give her more coffee' then elected to give Evelyn a sleeping tablet in an attempt to subdue her. And did it work? *No, it did not.* Not even close. Evelyn with two cups of coffee on board was out of control, and I had been an enabler, even if technically by default. I didn't seem to have much natural flair for this business.

Eventually another nurse turned up with some morphine, and Evelyn found her semi-stoned happy place. She stopped shrieking and rocking, and took a 20-minute nap while I tried to relax and returned to reading my book.

When Evelyn woke up, something had happened to her personality. Coherency was no longer a problem, but apparently I was. And she *looked* so sweet.

'I hate you,' she said.

'What?' I stared at her, and she looked me right in the eye, unblinking.

'I *said*, I hate you,' she repeated.

'How can you hate me? You don't even know me,' I replied.

'I know that I hate you,' she said. 'That's all I need to know.'

I tried not to laugh. 'Okay, Evelyn, you hate me. Sure.'

'I *hate* you.'

'Yeah, yeah, I got it.'

Evelyn coolly reached for her television remote, put the news on and watched it in silence. If I glanced over at her, she glared at me. But when the tea lady came into the room to deliver supper, Evelyn was as nice as pie.

'Cup of tea or coffee, love?' the woman asked.

'Coffee please, dear.' Evelyn smiled.

I put the kibosh on that quick smart. Evelyn was displeased, but since she already hated me, I wasn't particularly crushed by her fresh contempt. When the end of my shift finally rolled around at ten thirty, I practically skipped out of there. *So long, Evelyn! Don't go breaking a hip!* It wasn't the most heart-warming interaction of my life.

★

On my second shift as an AIN, I was lumped with supervision of a patient once again. This guy, Thahn, was 23 and dim as an environmentally friendly light bulb, but it wasn't really his fault. He had been found floating face-down in a creek, unconscious and not breathing, after he had whacked up some particularly pure heroin and rolled off the rocky ledge he was sitting on into the water. Hypoxia was nobody's friend and a brain starved of oxygen could be a one-way ticket to Shitsville. Depending on how long you went without, you could be left vegetable-like or a complete vegetable or brain dead. When Thahn was pulled out of the creek he was clinically dead, but the paramedics managed to bring him back. Well, they brought *most* of him back.

He was stuck in a general medical ward now, after a stint in the Intensive Care Unit, where he was hooked up to a battery of monitors while the extent of his brain damage was ascertained. He had a hole in his throat where the tracheostomy had been, but otherwise looked in reasonably good shape, apart from his forearms being furrowed with track marks so deep they looked like they had been made by a plough.

'What's your name?' he asked me, when I told him I was going to be looking after him for the afternoon.

'Kristy,' I said.

'You a nurse?' he asked.

'Kind of. I'm studying to be a nurse. I'm a Nursing Assistant at the moment.'

'Oh.'

He stared out the window, scratching absentmindedly

at a spot on his leg, so I figured we were done with the formalities. I started looking through his chart. It was a very thick volume for a 23-year-old, and that was always a bad sign.

Long-term intravenous drug user, primarily heroin and amphetamines. First use aged 13 . . . Extensive forensic history for breaking and entering, burglary, fraud and drug charges . . . Extremely compromised venous access . . . requires cannulation by guided ultrasound . . . History of numerous previous overdoses.

Substantial jail time, shitty veins, hepatitis C; it was the typical junkie trajectory, minus the predictably unhappy ending so far, but he was creeping ever closer to his swan song. Thahn's parents had migrated to Australia from Ho Chi Minh City when he was four years old and I doubted this was the auspicious future they had envisioned for him: heroin overdoses and speed sores, and almost eating it in a dirty creek where shopping trolleys rusted to death.

Thahn had physically detoxed from opiates over the last month while he was intubated and ventilated in Intensive Care, so he didn't have an *active* drug dependence, but his newly acquired brain injury wasn't exactly trading up.

He interrupted my reading. 'What's your name?'

'Kristy,' I told him again, and this time I showed him the name and photo on my nursing agency laminate. I thought that seeing it written down might help him retain the information. He looked down at the photo on my badge, and then back up at me.

'Are you a nurse?' he asked

'Yeah, I'm a sort of nurse,' I told him, nodding. 'See

here where it says "Assistant In Nursing"? That's the kind of nurse I am. I'm still learning.'

'You got any smokes?'

'Ah, no, I don't. Sorry.'

'I'll get one from my friend,' he said, walking out into the corridor, and I followed closely behind, like the endorsed stalker I was. He was allowed to visit the outdoor smoking area as long as someone was with him at all times, because he wandered. He couldn't remember where he was, or where he had come from, or where he was going, or why he was going there. Everything was a mystery to Thahn, and every 15 minutes it was a mystery all over again. Parts of his brain had died when he did, and once gone, they were gone forever, just like your virginity, or goodwill for a douchebag ex-lover. Now Thahn's brain was littered with little pockets of nothing, like Swiss cheese, or an Aero bar, which made me sad. And also made me hungry.

Thahn started to veer down the hallway towards the kitchen, the opposite direction to where he wanted to go.

'This way,' I told him, pointing towards the exit, and he changed course dumbly like a wind-up toy hitting a wall, performing a rather clumsy 180 but shuffling off in the right direction.

We walked outside into the glaring sunshine of the smoking area, which consisted of a picnic table and benches, all chained to the ground, in a cement square surrounded by a high wire fence. I imagined this was what jail would be like, but with more exercise equipment and sodomy. A rusty International Roast coffee tin sat on the middle of the table as an ashtray, overflowing with cigarette butts that had been smoked right down to the filter.

Thahn scavenged a cigarette from a fat, balding man in an ill-fitting Bon Jovi t-shirt who had a marked tremor *and* a tic, and whose hairy belly was spilling over the band of his shorts. Everything about him screamed *I am a mental health patient*. I was afraid to say anything in case he took it as an invitation to engage in conversation, because a 'chat' with a lonely mental health patient could make your brain bleed. Silence and a polite nod of the head was the safest option if you didn't want to get sucked into a conversational vacuum to rival a black hole. He lit a Holiday Extra Mild for Thahn, who smoked it the way a dog eats food, and immediately asked for another. The Fat Man obliged.

'Why are you in hospital?' the Fat Man quizzed Thahn.

'I lost a piece of my mind,' he said, which was a pretty succinct explanation.

Thahn sucked his second cigarette down mechanically. After a minute he looked at me. I was sitting across the picnic table from him, peacefully copping his passive smoke and squinting as the sun bounced off the concrete and burnt into my retinas, wishing I had thought to bring sunglasses with me.

'What's your name?' he asked me, like I was a person he had never seen before.

'It's still Kristy,' I said.

'Are you a nurse?'

Oh, for fuck's sake . . . It was a very long day.

Zoe

The third, and final, year of my nursing degree had the longest clinical placements, which was great if you liked the wards you were sent to and terrible if you didn't. I went to a couple of general medical wards in the first half of the year. They didn't exactly set my world on fire, but neither did they fill me with dread. The same could not be said of my final three-month placement on a Neurology and Stroke Unit, which I loathed.

In the last few months of study, I had to come up with my top three preferences for a graduate position. I was well schooled on where I *didn't* want to work, which was pretty much every place I had done a clinical placement or worked a shift as an AIN to date, but I had no idea where I *would* like to work, or if such a place even existed. Getting a real job, with real money, was the reason I had just spent three years writing essays about things and processes I had little interest in and now meaningful employment was right around the corner, but first I had to choose somewhere to be an employee. On a whim I applied for the Bone Marrow Transplant Unit. I chose it because of all the department names on the list for graduate positions, I thought it sounded the most interesting, and even a little exotic and exciting compared to Urology or Respiratory Medicine. At the time the extent of my knowledge of bone marrow transplant was only that it was a form of treatment for leukaemia, and all I knew of leukaemia was that Sadako from the book *Sadako and the Thousand Paper Cranes* had died from it after the atomic bombing of Hiroshima in 1945. I didn't know if I would like Bone Marrow Transplant, or if it would like me, but I was hopeful that there would be less shit eating and finger painting than on the Neurology and Stroke Ward because having to brush poo out of someone's teeth first thing in the morning was revolting.

I wrote an application, mostly lifted from my brother's application of the year before, attended an interview and found out a few weeks later that I had a full-time job, starting in two months' time. I hadn't even set foot on the ward prior to my first day, so I had no idea what was waiting for me, but knowing would not have helped at all.

The first week at the hospital was one of the dullest of my life, a long and tedious orientation with mandatory content on occupational health and safety issues and hospital protocol. The speakers were euthanising, the sandwiches were soggy and the coffee was International Roast, which tasted like arse. To add insult to injury, I was given my new uniform. It consisted of a fugly blue-and-white floral dress that people called the 'Libra Fleur' because it looked like the outside of a tampon box, a shirt in the same foul material, and navy slacks for cooler weather. I had each piece in duplicate. All three parts of the uniform weren't merely aesthetically offensive, they were also made of the cheapest synthetic fabric ever produced by Taiwan, so you would end up with big sweat patches under your arms or anywhere else your suffocating torso managed to produce moisture.

I took my hideous costume in hand, tried it on in the privacy of my own home, and had a full-blown temper tantrum. The dress was matronly and sack-like, the shirt somehow puffed up around the shoulders and made you look like a hunchback, and the slacks were so unforgiving that your arse should have come with flashing lights and a *Caution Wide Load* sign. The 'sexy nurse' stereotype had been debunked in one fell swoop. It was hideous, and I was contractually obliged to wear it. *In public.* I swore my head off, screwed each piece up into a ball and angrily launched them across the room, where they lay crumpled in the corner for the rest of the week. If I was going to be forced to wear things that gross, then they were going to be crushed and uncared for, at the very least.

When I turned up to the first day on the ward in my civilian clothes for another round of orientation, although this time transplant-specific, the scowl I had been wearing for a week instantly changed to a triumphant grin. Nurses were wearing light blue scrubs as far as the eye could see, and my vain brat prayer had been answered. I had dodged the ugly 'Libra Fleur' bullet after all, and I was basically going to be wearing *pyjamas* at work every day. It seemed I had somehow fallen arse backwards into the best job ever without even trying.

Unfortunately, my euphoria was short-lived. Beyond the coup of the scrubs were the patients, and they did not look like any other patients I had ever seen. Ageless bald people wandered aimlessly up and down the corridor, pale and, without eyebrows or eyelashes, looking vaguely extraterrestrial. They pushed huge machines that lit up like Christmas trees and had spaghetti junctions of tubing going in every direction. Assorted bags and bottles of liquid hung from metal branches with machinery stacked upon more machinery and it all beeped loudly and often. It looked very complicated and overwhelming, and it was. I began to panic.

Zoe was the first patient I met on the ward, and she was kind of a bitch to me, but she was a bitch to everyone else, too. I had to learn how to collect blood from the catheter in her arm, under close supervision, and she wasn't impressed that she was going to be used as a teaching prop. She had only just arrived on the ward and, when I approached with a bunch of syringes and tubes, said, unsmilingly, 'I hope you know what you're doing.'

I didn't say anything. I had *no idea* what I was doing but I wasn't about to admit it. I didn't even know how I had ended up in this alien ward in the first place; I may as well have thrown a dart at a map of the hospital. So Zoe and I were both strangers to this complex world of PICC lines and implanted ports and Hickman's catheters, to constant extractions of blood and injection of drugs, and we were both petrified and in shock. I got to leave at the end of the day though, and didn't have leukaemia, so I cut Zoe some slack. I would have been angry if I were in her slippers, too. After a few days, her frosty attitude thawed and my terror subsided slightly, and we both began to slowly settle into our new home.

A month earlier, Zoe had celebrated her 40th birthday, and gotten engaged. She had a ten-year-old son from a previous relationship and had been feeling increasingly tired and run down, so her doctor sent her for a blood test. She was excited because she thought she was pregnant, and instead she was told that she had acute myeloid leukaemia. Her dad had died of the same disease in his late forties, which made her diagnosis even more devastating. Zoe had been busy renovating her house and making wedding plans one day, and the next found herself in a starched hospital bed, scared shitless and looking down the barrel of chemotherapy.

Zoe busted everybody's balls for the first month, demanding to know what was going in and out of her IV lines at all times, and why we needed to take blood *again*, which I guess was her attempt to feel some semblance of control in a completely out-of-control situation. Then she started to relax, and it turned out she was my kind of person: loud, crude and funny. I always seemed to be looking after her section of the ward, and we had a good rapport, more like friendship than servitude. She had a lot of spirit, was also a big fan of alcohol and swore as much as I did, although I tried to keep a lid on it at work.

'Oh, that's *fucked*! I spent a fortune on this shit!' Zoe complained, when the doctor explained that she could expect her bleached blonde hair to start falling out in the very near future as the chemotherapy took hold. And she was pissed off because she wouldn't be able to have sex with her fiancé when she became cytotoxic from all the cancer-killing drugs, as the poisonous chemicals would wash out of her body in her sweat and any other secretions.

'You know what? This leukaemia thing is a pile of fucking shit!' she said to me, bitterly, one afternoon, when her son came to visit her after school and she was told by the doctors that she couldn't give him a hug or a kiss because of the high risk of infection. She went ahead and did it anyway.

There wasn't much I could say to comfort her. It was shitty, cruel and unfair, but cancer just is.

Zoe got used to the routine after a little while. She sailed through her first cycle of chemo and went home, her hair, beginning to shed, left behind on the pillow.

She came back for her second round and this time went home bald as an egg, but was less scared because she knew what to expect. It wasn't fun, but it was the same nurses, the same doctors, the same crappy food, the same everything.

She was re-admitted unexpectedly a week after the second cycle, because she had spiked a temperature to 39.2°C and she was neutropenic, which meant that she had no good cells left to fight infection and would need a course of intravenous antibiotics.

I was about to finish my shift, so I went to say goodbye and Zoe asked if I could get her a toothbrush and some toothpaste. She hadn't counted on coming back in so suddenly and her fiancé couldn't bring the rest of her things until the morning.

'You're my favourite nurse, you know that?' she said when I gave them to her.

'Oh, thanks.' I blushed, feeling embarrassed. 'Well, I'll see you on Sunday, I'm on days off now.'

'Okay, girl! You behave yourself!' she said, winking at me.

I told her I would try.

I had two days off, did something leisurely, I'm sure, most likely drinking until drunk because that was what I did for entertainment, and then I was back at work on Sunday afternoon for the late shift. The atmosphere on the ward was sombre. Zoe's mother and sister and fiancé were hovering around one of the single rooms at the front of the ward now, crying and hugging each other in the corridor. If you got moved to one of the front rooms, you were in deep shit.

'What happened?' I asked one of the stony-faced nurses at the front desk. Usually when you turned up to work, someone was laughing or joking around or cheerfully greeting the arrival of the next shift and imminent freedom, but this day was different. It was eerily quiet, and everybody looked miserable.

'Zoe had a bleed.'

On Saturday evening Zoe had staggered down the hall, looking like she was stoned or drunk, and had been barely able to stand. The nurses thought that she was over-sedated, that maybe they had given her too much morphine, so they got her back into bed, phoned the doctor and before anyone could review her, she began spiralling into unconsciousness.

Platelets are like glue, the cells that hold blood together in its usual slightly viscous state, and when they are low, blood thins and spills freely. A healthy number of platelets for the average person is between 150,000 and 400,000 per micro litre, so if you cut yourself when you're cooking, or fall down and skin your knee, your blood will clot and stop you bleeding to death. Zoe had a platelet count of 5,000 when her brain began to bleed spontaneously, and for no apparent reason, so there was nothing to impede the flood. It was hopeless. Everybody was upset, her family and the staff and the other patients.

It took a whole day for her to die, even though from the moment she lost consciousness she wasn't going to wake up again. When she finally died around nine o'clock, her son's screaming rang out through the entire ward and chilled blood to ice.

The first dead person I'd seen was on my third day on the ward. Alarms blared and lights started flashing and I followed the commotion to a front room. An old lady had gone into cardiac arrest, and I watched CPR being given, and adrenaline, and all of that shit, to no avail. She died anyway.

I said, 'Is that it?' People looked at me, other nurses and doctors who had seen it all before, and someone answered, 'Yep, that's it.' I went out for a drink after my shift, and I kept thinking, *Is that it?* because it felt like there should be something more, that you shouldn't just disappear from life, but you do, and Zoe's disappearance really hurt.

I didn't want to be alone after work the night Zoe died, so I took a taxi to my best friend's house and picked up a six-pack of beer on the way. I had an early shift in the morning and I didn't want to go back, *ever*. I talked a lot and cried a little, and drank until I achieved some degree of numbness.

When I turned up to work the next morning, bleary eyed and drained, Zoe's name had been erased from the board and her room was clean and empty, like she was never there and it had all been a bad dream. And that just made it worse.

Sheila

The prospect of becoming a shift worker didn't really faze me because I spent a lot of time staying up all night when I was studying, either because I had only just started the assignment that was due in the next morning, or I was out making money for rent and food at my white-trash bar job. The bar was an inner-city shithole that had once had a Sinatra-style swing band that drew in a large number of middle-aged clientele, but the owner decided that his bar could do perfectly well without paying the band's overinflated fee, thank you very much, and he effectively shot himself in the foot. The band left, the customers followed and the business slowly died. Employees who left were never replaced, and eventually I was the only girl working behind the bar, so whenever some pissed chick yakked up in the ladies toilets, I was lumped with the job of scooping the bright pink Vodka Cruiser and pizza puke out of the blocked sink, or mopping it off the floor. Staying up all night cleaning up other people's vomit – it wasn't that dissimilar to nursing, really, except for the incredibly loud music and everyone being drunk. I figured night duty at the hospital would be a breeze.

For the first few months as a Registered Nurse, we were sheltered from nights and only worked day shifts. I eventually found, to my horror, that night shift at the hospital was nothing like staying up drinking and smoking after closing time at the bar. I was excited for an hour or two on the first night, because it sort of felt like I was at a slumber party, in scrubs that looked and felt like pyjamas, filling up on junk food. Everyone got a bit silly and giggly at night, including the patients, who were full of pharmaceuticals and free-balling cancer cells and were being woken every thirty minutes by beeping machinery and blood pressure cuffs or an urgent need to vomit, piss, shit or, worse, all three at once. Everybody was a little delirious, and at first it was almost fun.

The novelty of night shift wore off fast, though, and so did the coffee. I drank so much of it my stomach churned and I ended up with a cracking headache. I was 15 different kinds of tired, awake when my body knew better, and the whole thing felt like swimming against a rip.

At three am I was dehydrated, depressed and nauseated. I voiced my dismay to my co-workers.

'This isn't *at all* like staying up all night drinking!' I complained.

'No, it certainly isn't,' the older nurses agreed. Everyone

hated night shift, but they had hated it for a lot longer than I had. My disappointment was painfully raw.

We worked in teams in Bone Marrow, and tiredness does not bring out the social butterfly in me, so if I was paired up with a chatty nurse, I was just about homicidal after an hour. I buried my head in a book or patients' charts, put my iPod on and emitted antisocial signals like a flashing beacon at sea, and some people *still* didn't pick up on it.

'. . . so my boyfriend . . . and I said to Simone . . .'

And going through my head on a continuous loop was *Die, already. Just die.*

If it was a quiet night and nobody was bothering me, I would run through all the things I would give up if I could just shut my eyes and go to sleep, as if such a trading scheme existed outside of my own feverish, oblivion-craving brain.

Sense of smell? Yeah, I'll trade it. That could be quite an advantage around here.

Eyesight, no. And not hearing or taste either.

Sexual favours definitely, but nothing top shelf . . .

I would also hatch plans to get a new job, or think of ways to downsize my life, my wants and whims, in order to never have to do night duty again. *I'll just watch a documentary on Mexico, then I wouldn't have to be here, doing this. I'll stop going out for drinks, and eating, and living in a house . . .* And then a patient would ring their buzzer, and even though I didn't want to get up and answer it, I had to, and the spell of tiredness and self-pity was broken, if only for a short time. Meanwhile, my sick and dying patients steadfastly went about their business of being sick and dying. Nobody was winning in this particular neck of the woods.

By the time the first round of morning observations arrived, my stomach was sick of having coffee and tea poured into it and I hated all of my patients, even the nice ones. A decent amount of the meanness was mine, but the rest of it was night shift's fault. I usually asked the patients how they had slept, too brain dead to think of any other topic of conversation, and inevitably someone complained, 'Terrible! I hardly slept a wink! This mattress is like a *rock*!' which spawned mutinous fantasies of me reefing them out and crawling in myself, with an added punch in the mouth for being ungrateful.

The fact that I was building violent castles in the air centred on beating up cancer patients was a bit of a red flag that night duty and I were not a good fit, and also that I was not a very nice person, which for some reason surprised people. Most people assume that if you're a nurse, you're a good person, which is unrealistic and a bit mental, but it's much better than having people automatically assume you're a boring prick because you work in accounting.

Adrenaline, sugar and saturated fat kept me going until seven thirty, when I crashed after handover to the day staff, dog-tired and delirious and miserable at the thought of having to do it all over again the next night, and the next, and the next . . . I had jetlag and no duty-free booze, photos or fun memories to show for it, and my skin was so parched it felt like my face was going to split in half. My whole life and everything in it just *sucked*. When I finally fell into my own bed at eight thirty in the morning, I was the furthest from the next night shift I could be, with nothing to do but rest, and it almost made everything okay again. At that moment I loved sleep so much I would marry it, and I've never loved anyone that much.

Everything is exaggerated at night, the good and the bad. I have seriously considered jumping out of a window on night duty. And other times I have never laughed so hard in my life.

This particular night began at seven and I was looking after Sheila. At seven thirty-five she tried to punch me but I ducked out of the way just in time and she only ended up clipping me slightly. She was pushing 80 and had end-stage cancer, although it seemed she hadn't gotten the memo, because it didn't look like she was going anywhere anytime soon, and she had a pretty impressive swing for someone at death's door. Sheila was typically as placid as a lamb, but when her kidneys started to back up and her bloodstream filled with toxic garbage, her oxygen levels dropped and she got a little loose, which ran the gamut from disobedience and bad language all the way to fisticuffs and nudity.

Ordinarily Sheila had no issue with wearing a hospital gown, but this was not one of those times. And she hadn't merely discarded her clothing, she had also pulled down both her IV lines and thrown all her sheets, blankets and both her pillows on the floor while she lay back in bed, naked as the day she was born and laughing her head off. She seemed to be enjoying herself, at least, but I wasn't loving our evening together quite so much. It was my responsibility to check her observations regularly and administer the myriad drugs she needed, which was difficult as there was no venous access and Sheila refused to open her mouth whenever I came near her with a glass of water and a cupful of pills.

By midnight Sheila was barking commands, hurling abuse and giggling non-stop. She wanted a cigarette and a gin and tonic, and she wanted it *now*.

'Yeah, well, that makes two of us,' I said, and she roared with laughter, which was extra contagious when combined with my rapidly accelerating fatigue. Every time she laughed, I started laughing, and a few times I had to step outside of the room to get a grip and rest my aching face and stomach muscles while she hurled threats after me and cackled like a witch.

'Come back here, you *whooore*! I'll box your ears! *Ahahahahahahaha!*'

Sheila let me stick a thermometer in her mouth, but only because she thought it was a cigarette holder, which was a lucky break for me. I had given up trying to take her axillary temperature – sticking the thermometer under her arm – because twice she let it sit there for a few seconds, lulling me into a false sense of security before she suddenly grabbed it and launched it at the window, and when I tried to use a tympanic thermometer – the kind you stick in your ear – she slapped my arm away, greatly annoyed, and shouted, 'BUZZ OFF!' This thermometer she just chomped down on like Groucho Marx with a cigar, and when it beeped and I could finally wrestle it out from between her teeth, her temperature was 39.4°C. So it was really no wonder she kept throwing off the covers and getting nude.

I called the doctor to get her reviewed, because a high temperature combined with a poorly functioning immune system usually meant antibiotics, or any other treatment to curtail whatever kind of infection was present.

The doctor, a young intern, was a bit shocked when she tapped on the door at four thirty and entered Sheila's room to find the patient sitting up in bed buck naked, wide awake and grinning like a loon.

'Fuckity!' Sheila shrieked. 'Fuckity, fuckity, *fuck*!'

The doctor introduced herself and told Sheila that she needed to have a listen to her chest with a stethoscope. Sheila was not impressed, and wrinkled her nose like she smelled dog shit.

'You're mealy-mouthed,' she haughtily informed the doctor, 'and mealy-mouthed people aren't allowed to touch me.'

The doctor stared and I burst out laughing. It seemed like a good time to go on a tea-break.

Sheila was trying to bargain with me. She had agreed to swallow a couple of Panadol to bring her temperature down, which she crunched between her yellow teeth like peppermints, grimacing, and then refused to wash down with water. But she wasn't going to let me check her blood pressure again unless I gave her a cigarette.

'Sorry, Sheila, I can't.'

'Can't, or *won't*?' She arched an eyebrow at me.

'Both,' I told her, and she immediately drew her arms in tight, hugging herself, so I couldn't put the cuff on either of her arms. Sheila's hair was white but stained orange around her face, like rust, from 60 years of heavy smoking. I slapped another nicotine patch on the bit of her arm she would let me touch, but a patch was a far cry from a cigarette, so it wasn't shit to Sheila.

The doctor didn't think she was going to last much longer, because the blood tests showed her kidneys were failing – everything was failing – but to look at her, so feisty and nuts and naked, it was difficult to believe she would succumb to anything, out of stubbornness alone.

'Come on, Sheila. Be nice to me. It's six in the morning and I'm tired,' I said, holding the flaccid blood pressure cuff in my hand like a limp dick.

Sheila grinned at me, eyes bright and wide.

'EAT SHIT!' she yelled suddenly, and laughed uproariously.

Eat shit, indeed. Some nights it's all you do.

Shit

Speaking of shit, it was three in the morning, and another nurse, Amanda, and I were cleaning Patricia up. She was on the way out and suffering from the dreaded double incontinence – loss of bladder and bowel function at the same time – which was par for the course when you were dying of cancer. We had just finished putting clean sheets on the bed when Patricia suddenly sat up and yelled out, 'DANGER! DANGER! STAND BACK!'

If Patricia wasn't about to have a heart attack, then Amanda and I were. We both jumped back from the bed – and practically out of our skin – in fright.

'What is it?' I asked, alarmed, just as another black river of shit poured out of her onto the freshly made bed. On the one hand, I was relieved it was diarrhoea, and on the other hand, I was devastated it was diarrhoea.

'I'm *so* sorry!' she said, starting to laugh. Patricia was completely delirious from exhaustion, lack of sleep and the fact that she was slowly fading, and soon we were all giggling because we were running on fumes, too. It was the kind of laughter that you have no control over, and if you've ever cleaned up a puddle of shit in the middle of the night on zero sleep, then you'll know what I'm talking about. Better laughter than tears, though, because at three in the morning and on our fourth bed change and counting, it really could have gone either way.

I felt bad for patients when they apologised for bodily processes that were beyond their control. I tried to reassure them and say it was no big deal, although it was for them, of course. Nobody in their right mind would ever *choose* to be that vulnerable, or to suffer the indignity of having your arse wiped as an adult, but it happened. And no matter how gross it might be – and it was really rank sometimes – it was my job to deal with the mess and, at the very least, make light of it. I could complain all I wanted when I got home from work, and believe me I did, because when I said 'work was shit', I often meant it literally.

It had been a long night, but they always were. I walked into the bedroom and sat on the edge of the bed, in a haze. My boyfriend was getting dressed for his day job, like a normal person, while I was about to crawl under the covers and sleep the day away and have breakfast cereal for dinner when I woke up.

'Hey, there's chocolate on your shoe,' my boyfriend said, and I looked down at my feet and sighed. Well, this was just *wonderful*.

'It's not chocolate,' I told him, as I carefully removed my shoe and tried to avoid touching the stain. Even though we wore scrubs and plastic aprons and gloves and masks, we didn't usually cover our feet, so I occasionally brought my 'work' home with me. I dropped my shoe into the bin. They had been my favourite pair of work shoes, too, and now they were just my favourite work shoe.

'What are you doing?' my boyfriend asked, frowning at my wasteful disposal of footwear, then recoiled with a disgusted '*Oh my god!*' when he realised that my shoe was not decorated with anything as lovely as dessert. I worked in a *hospital*, for Christ's sake, not a restaurant, so it couldn't really have been anything else. My boyfriend looked traumatised. He would never have made it as a nurse, and I wouldn't have wanted him to, either. One person bringing other people's faeces home was plenty for one household.

I never really thought of poo in its many various guises until 2005, when I got gastro in a developing country. Then I began working full-time in a hospital, where other people's business became my business. If I wasn't emptying it out of a pan or wiping it off someone, I was asking patients if they'd 'moved their bowels today' and if so, how many times, while querying the consistency and colour of their output. I was basically a poo detective, however reluctantly I carried out my duties, because other people's crap was like other people's children: you were never going to like them as much as your own.

When a buzzer went off in one of the patient bathrooms, it was usually because an IV had started beeping when a bag of fluid had finished running through, or someone had gotten tangled up trying to get undressed for the shower with all the tubes connected to them threaded through the sleeves of their pyjamas. One of my patient's buzzers had gone off, and the light above the furthest bathroom door was flashing, so I walked down the corridor and knocked on the door.

'You okay in there?' I called out, and the answer was a resounding, 'NO!'

I opened the door quickly, and gasped. My patient, John, was sitting on the toilet with a horrified look on his face and his pyjama pants bunched around his ankles. I didn't understand how it was possible, but bright yellow-coloured shit was *everywhere*. His diarrhoea had splattered like a dropped bucket of paint, as if someone had stuck a firecracker up his arse and lit it. There was shit spattered over every visible surface, the walls, the shower curtain, and all over the toilet. It was every place except where it was meant to be. It was *incredible*. Not Seven Wonders of the World incredible, but it was a shit spectacle unlike any other I had ever seen, that's for sure.

'*Oh my god!*' I exclaimed, and the patient shook his head in bewilderment. 'How . . . how did it . . .?' I stammered. What the hell had happened in here?

'I don't know,' he said, dismayed. 'I just leant over to pull my shorts down and my bum, just sort of–' he motioned at the mayhem '–*exploded*.'

We looked around the room, both of us shocked and awed, and then we started to laugh. There wasn't really any other option. I went to get him some towels and fresh pyjamas, and directed him to the next bathroom so he could have a shower and sort himself out, and then I paged the cleaner. This was an industrial-sized job, and it was going to take much more than a few handfuls of paper towels to mop it up. I didn't want John to feel bad, or embarrassed about his 'accident', so I tried to be mature and stop giggling, but I was dying on the inside.

As I was walking back down the corridor, my friend Eileen saw me smiling and asked me what was so funny. So I took her to the soiled bathroom and pushed the door open with my foot. Her jaw dropped.

'*Oh my god!*' she blurted, her eyes widening in shock as she took in the full scope of the disaster. 'What *happened*?'

I couldn't answer her, because I was too busy falling on the floor, laughing, and Eileen lost it, too, but when the cleaner arrived with her mop and bucket and a large trolley of cleaning products, she didn't find it funny at all.

At the opposite end of the poo spectrum from diarrhoea was manual evacuation, and I was more afraid of it than most things in hospital, and probably more than most things in life.

When a patient complained of constipation, there were a couple of necessary points of investigation. You checked what bowel-stupefying medications they might be taking, like opiates for pain relief, which automatically threw their innards into slow gear. You asked your patient if they were eating, and if there was actually stuff going in that you could reasonably expect to turn up at the other end sometime. And you needed to make sure that your patient was keeping hydrated and that their poo hadn't just dried up and lodged in situ because lack of fluids had turned it into a pebble.

To resolve constipation, stool softeners like Coloxyl, or Coloxyl & Senna, would be prescribed. Hopefully that would be enough to get the party started, but if not, you could try a sticky drink of Lactulose, or even Movicol, a powder that turned into a claggy glue when you added water and was meant to sweep through the bowel like a flash flood, clearing everything in its path.

If there was still no 'movement', and your patient's abdomen was bloated and distended to the point that they looked pregnant, then the doctor might request a 'manual evacuation'. Such a directive was often followed, conveniently, by the doctor being paged to attend a medical emergency elsewhere in the hospital. The nurses were left to do the dirty work, and it was literally the dirtiest work around.

This is the point at which you would have seen me running out of the hospital, screaming, to avoid donning gloves lubricated with KY Jelly and indulging in gentle exploration and coaxing out, or even breaking up, of wayward faeces. During this mutually unpleasant process you tried to preserve the dignity of your poor, uncomfortable patient, and wondered how your life had come to this, a couple of fingers up somebody else's bum *and* they hadn't even bought you a drink first.

Sarah

Sarah was 16 and had recently been diagnosed with biphenotypic leukaemia. Granted, leukaemia itself was brutal enough, but if you added the word 'biphenotypic' to it, something that was already intrinsically bad was made a whole lot worse, like poorly performed musical theatre with tone-deaf hammy actors. If you added something called the 'Philadelphia Chromosome' to the equation, which Sarah *also* had, you were so deeply in shit that you might as well bathe in sewage and drink from your toilet. Leukaemia is a complicated disease to explain but put simply, Sarah's cancer was rare with an additional chromosomal abnormality that made it exceptionally difficult to treat.

There were a lot of different strains of leukaemia, all broken up into categories and sub-categories, depending on the kind of cells they originated from and how quickly they were developing. New kinds were being discovered all the time, which was disheartening, but the more that was learnt about the disease, the more refined the chemical warfare produced to destroy it became. The host now had a fighting chance of surviving the treatment, if not the actual disease.

As a rule, acute leukaemia progressed more rapidly than the slowly smouldering chronic types. Without prompt intervention, both would kill you in the end, but it was either the hare or the tortoise that was carrying you to the finishing line. Sarah's leukaemia was acute, so she wasn't just sick, she was also getting sicker faster. Some people have all the luck. 'Philadelphia positive biphenotypic leukaemia' was hard to say, and terrible to have. There was a degree of hope, because there's always hope, but it was so minuscule in Sarah's case, it was hardly worth mentioning.

I don't remember how long the interval was between her coming in to hospital and it becoming obvious that she wouldn't be leaving again, but it was a pretty small window. Sarah was admitted to the Transplant Unit with blonde hair to her shoulders, a newly inserted Hickman's catheter in her chest wall, and an appropriate amount of fear and nervousness for a 16-year-old with a deadly illness. She was trying to be positive, despite an underlying abject terror. A bone marrow transplant was a huge, frightening gamble, but it was her only chance of survival.

The 16-year-old *me*, meanwhile, was a healthy, selfish, self-indulgent turd, concerned with important things like boys, being 'cool', badmouthing my parents and sneaking cigarettes and alcohol wherever possible. Sarah didn't even get the opportunity to show the world what a jerk she could be, or to then outgrow the mandatory jerk phase and eventually emerge resembling a somewhat decent human being from the cold war of adolescence. It may not *sound* like a great loss, but it was. She deserved to act like a petulant arsehole for years; it was every teenager's divine right. Instead, she was catapulted backwards to an ever more vulnerable extension of childhood, with an aggressive leukaemia nobody could better with a cure or a kiss.

The cocktail of drugs Sarah was given kept her up all night, as did the relentless activity of her gut. She had constant diarrhoea, and was growing thinner and weaker after only ten days in hospital. She would watch television in the middle of the night, when there was nothing but nonstop infomercials and the constant intrusion of night duty nurses to keep her company. It wasn't much of a social life.

I knocked on the door of her room at four am. We had to take blood from her Hickman line so the doctors could check her levels, and find out if she needed a blood transfusion that day. We were topping her up with the red blood cells and platelets that her body produced only in negligible amounts.

'Anything good on?' I asked, as Sarah's ghostly pale skin flickered by the light of the television.

'No,' Sarah said, disgustedly. 'It's so stupid. People who don't need to lose weight are selling exercise equipment, and people with good skin are selling pimple cream. It's retarded!'

I laughed, and she smiled.

A short time later, the focus of Sarah's treatment

switched, and it became about buying her time and keeping her as comfortable as possible, until the inevitable occurred. Sadly, there was minimal success on either front.

She went downhill fast, which is how it usually goes, and while there's no good way for a 16-year-old to die, a decreased period of suffering was preferable to something long and drawn out. It was vaguely more humane for Sarah, although that wasn't much consolation for her family.

I went away on holidays for two weeks and when I came back, I was looking after Sarah on night duty again, but there was scarcely any resemblance between the Sarah I had known and the one I was seeing now. She looked younger and older at the same time. She seemed more vulnerable and childlike, but she was tired and worn out with dark shadows under her eyes. Sleep remained excruciatingly elusive. She was so exhausted she burst into tears all the time, in addition, of course, to knowing that she was never going home. Too frail to get out of bed, she had a catheter inserted in her bladder and a bag of dark red-tinted pee hung from the bedrail beside her. There were adult-sized nappies for the diarrhoea, and we cleaned her up the best we could when things got messy. It was heartbreaking. The television was switched off.

On my last 12-hour night shift of three, Sarah was terrified and panting like an injured animal. Her body was struggling to keep up with itself. It seemed like every ten minutes she was doubled over as her bowel leached black blood, purging dead tissue and cellular waste. The smell was horrible and metallic, like an abattoir floor instead of a hospital.

'Am I going to die?' she asked me, gripping my hand with her eyes opened wide, begging for reassurance amid all the tubing and pain. Two enormous five-litre bags of saline were flowing through her catheter in continuous bladder irrigation, but huge blood clots kept forming there anyway, causing agonising spasms. Not even morphine was helping anymore, and there was a fine line between adequately medicating for her pain and depressing her critically weakened respiratory function with opiates. The margin for error was very narrow.

'No, Sarah, not tonight,' I said. I felt sick. It was the truth, sort of. I rubbed her back and tried to comfort her. She was going to die, but it probably wasn't going to happen tonight. For the moment, her vital signs were okay.

When I went on my break at three thirty, after hours of watching over her, I was exhausted, angry and upset. People talked about God and heaven a lot when someone died, finding comfort and reassurance in these concepts, but seeing death up close had the opposite effect on me. I was unconvinced there was a God, despite my Catholic upbringing and education, and if there *was* such a thing, then I was of the opinion that God was a proper bastard. Sarah was 16 and in here, dying and bleeding from everywhere, when she should have been at home, being a shithead teenager with her shithead teenage friends. I wanted to beat something up because this horror show was so unfair I could scream. Thankfully, not every shift was as awful and harrowing as this one had been.

'Are you okay?' my friend Allison asked, looking up from her magazine in the staffroom as I reached for a coffee cup and took the milk out of the fridge.

'No,' I told her. 'This job is really *fucked* sometimes. I hate it.'

'Yeah, it is,' she agreed, sadly. Some days, and nights, were just a pile of shit, and you couldn't do a thing about it.

We had already handed over our patients from the night shift to the morning staff when there was a shout from the hallway.

'She's crashing!'

Sarah's oxygen levels had suddenly plummeted on the change of staff. As a fresh crew of nurses from the day shift swarmed into the room, I phoned her mother and tried to convey a calm I didn't feel. I told her she needed to come to the hospital straightaway, that Sarah's condition was deteriorating but she was still here. Panic coursed through me and then I went numb. Once again, I had been cast in the role of 'The Nurse', who in this scene phoned the family and said, 'Come to the hospital! There's not a moment to lose!' I felt like I was stuck in a television show I hadn't signed up to be on, and it was a darkly depressing medical drama when all I wanted was laughs. Nothing seemed real.

'I'm leaving now.' Her mother sounded under control, and her tone was measured.

I suppose she had prepared herself, somehow, for a telephone call like this. The alarms sounded as Sarah's oxygen levels fell, from 70% to 58%, and the crash cart came flying into the room. Sarah's head was tilted back, a mask clamped firmly to her jaw so air could be manually pushed into her failing lungs. She was too unwell to cry, but she was scared witless. She had been on the ward long enough to know what the crash cart meant – someone was in big trouble, and this time it was *her* – and then she was unconscious.

'Go home and get some sleep,' one of the other nurses said. I was officially on days off, and while I didn't want to stay exactly, I didn't want to go either, but I walked away, heart pounding with the rush of adrenaline and my brain paralysed by shock. The medical intervention continued as my night duty buddy Darren and I went for a solemn breakfast at a café down the street, wide awake for our impromptu memorial. We guessed that Sarah would have passed away by the time we left the café, but she hung on for two more days, and finally died with her mum by her side, holding her hand and making it better.

The thing with patients that were going to die was that you couldn't actually believe it until it happened, and even then, you *still* couldn't believe it. You knew, intellectually, that the person who had uncontrollable bleeding and weakening vital signs was going to succumb to their illness long before it happened, but when it came to pass, it was still completely shocking. Each death was a sucker punch, and every sucker punch had the same effect on me: I went out and got really drunk. Alcohol had stopped being a luxury and become a necessity.

I don't know if the alcohol ever helped, exactly, but it usually made me forget what I was trying to forget. Or else it made me so sick that I could only think about how ill I was feeling, and *that* distracted me from thinking about whatever it was I had been endeavouring to forget. I had a system. It may not have been good for my brain or my liver or my bank account, but I found it adequately escapist and therapeutic.

Some weeks, two or three of the patients we had looked after for the last few years passed away, and sometimes within the same day. They seemed to catch wind of death, and followed each other, like women going to the toilet at a nightclub. Those times were rough, demoralising and emotionally draining. Conversely, there were also long, quiet lulls, weeks where people were safely discharged home and nobody died and the biggest threat, to patients and staff alike, was killer boredom. Some days were *too* calm, without even a hint of storm, and as a reward for surviving one of those monotonous marathons, you guessed it, I went out and got really drunk. My system was incredibly versatile. It also worked well at family events, weddings, Christmas, public holidays, all birthdays and Saturdays.

I drank a lot as a student/bartender, because it was just what you did at the end of a 12-hour shift: you stopped pouring drinks for other people and began pouring them for yourself. I enjoyed that part of bar work the most, the knock-off drinks where you got steaming drunk before falling into bed in broad daylight, but this was not that kind of drinking. It was medicinal, not social. Working in a bar may have given me an informal traineeship in drinking, but Oncology gave me a licence, with its ever-present themes of sorrow and loss.

Dennis

For people who work in the field of 'health', some of the unhealthiest people I have met are nurses. They have been some of the biggest drinkers, most prolific pharmaceutical abusers and rabid consumers of junk food I have ever known, and that's without mentioning those of seriously dubious mental health or the emotional cripples. Practising what you preach isn't compulsory, I guess, but it lends you a little more credibility to at least *act* the part of a 'health professional', by trying to disguise your own shortcomings. Coming back to a cancer or respiratory ward reeking from your latest cigarette break just makes you look like an ignorant arsehole.

Shift work could make healthy living a difficult undertaking, but it was great if you wanted to be addicted to caffeine or other instant sources of energy, and if possessing a decimated body clock was at all appealing. Add a stressful day of people bleeding, dying or just threatening to kick the shit out of you in the hospital car park, and you were also left fairly open to the idea of a stiff drink after work. If you were me, one drink usually became 100 drinks, and then you were obliged to attend your next shift despite feeling like you could vomit out of your eyes. My system wasn't entirely without its downside.

Generally speaking, turning up for work hungover was tolerated, although not appreciated, because it was better than not turning up at all and throwing the staffing completely out of whack. It always felt like the worst day of your life, though, and I usually spent it swearing that I would never mistreat myself in such a fashion ever again. Turning up to the hospital still intoxicated, however, was *really* uncool. I found that out the hard way, as I seem to be programmed to learn all of my lessons in life.

After a night out with friends spent drinking a ridiculous number of gin and tonics, I rolled home at five in the morning. If the bar hadn't closed, I would probably still be there now. I wrestled with my key in the door for about five minutes, then staggered upstairs and fell on to my bed. It was officially too late to call in 'sick' for the day – I was back on day shift – because phoning it in two hours before starting time incurred both the wrath of God *and* the Nurse Unit Manager. Calling in 'drunk' didn't seem like a viable option either. It was still dark outside, so I thought I could just sleep it off before work, despite my window for this only being the 45 minutes I had before my alarm went off.

Deep inside my drunken denial, I knew the sun was going to be rising over a world of pain, but I had almost convinced myself that a nap, a cold shower and strong coffee would be enough to make me presentable for work. And even when I fell out of the door of the taxi that dropped me off at the front of the hospital, I just thought it was funny. Then I giggled my way through morning handover and fought a strong urge to tell my co-workers that I loved them, and *that* was when I realised that I was actually *drunk, and at work*, and was about to enter a unique hell, of my own and Bombay Sapphire's making.

Being drunk at work is not nearly as much fun as it sounds. I went in to see my patient, Dennis, a 38-kilogram man with full-blown AIDS. He was sitting up in bed, a skeleton covered in mottled skin with tubes in every available orifice. He looked like death that had been warmed up and then left out in the sun for the buzzards to pick over.

'You look terrible!' he said, by way of a greeting, which was pretty funny, really, but I realised my lack of sleep and surplus of alcohol was a poorly kept secret.

'Thanks, Dennis, I'm not much of an early bird,' I replied.

'I'll say!' he agreed, a little too enthusiastically for my liking. Still, it wasn't often that Dennis got to feel like he was winning at something, and I was really more concerned with trying not to gag as I carried his dirty bedpan to the washer, feeling like I was on a boat. My stomach was queasy and I could already feel a headache coming on. If I felt this rough when I was still *drunk*, then I really needed to prepare myself for the impending comedown. I dished all of Dennis's morning drugs out into a little paper cup, then made one for myself with paracetamol and vitamins and anti-nausea tablets, in an attempt to head my galloping hangover off at the pass. I would have preferred to be self-medicating with sleep and a cheeseburger, or more booze, but drugs were much easier to come by in hospital.

Because he was so unwell I was going to be stuck looking after Dennis for the rest of the day with both of us looking and feeling like death, and that further sickened me for a couple of reasons. Dennis was in his mid forties and had spent a lot of time in Asia on unspecified 'business' over the years, but he had no qualms about voicing his disdain for 'those dirty nips'. He refused to let the Filipino cleaner enter his room because he 'couldn't be sure that she wouldn't steal something', even though the only thing worth stealing in his room was the medical equipment, and there was a hospital full of that stuff all around him that the cleaner had managed *not* to steal for the last ten years. Dennis had no manners to speak of, did not seem to have heard of the words 'please' or 'thank you', let alone possess an understanding of when they might be most appropriately used, and he also had mean little blackcurrants for eyes. I was not his biggest fan. Yes, he was dying and would do so imminently, and of course that was very sad and all, but a jerk was still a jerk, terminally ill or not. I had to look after him, but I didn't have to like him. My only obligation was to not let it show.

Dennis said he had no idea how he had contracted HIV, but that no doubt he had 'got it from an Asian'. The doctors said that he had probably been HIV positive for more than five years before he was tested, so when he finally came into hospital for treatment, very little could be done for him. He had been diagnosed at too late a stage for any of the standard treatments to be very effective. Initially, there was discussion of a possible bone marrow transplant, since his immune system was basically a blank slate, but that proposal vanished as his blood results deteriorated. It soon became a patch job on someone completely riddled with holes.

Because Dennis had been in hospital for a couple of months, he had his single room set up for convenience, customised the way he wanted it. There was a table next to his bed covered in half-eaten tubs of custard and jelly with dirty spoons sticking out of them, boxes of Dutch Chocolate Sustagen, and packets of lollies and crackers within arm's reach for snacking. Even though he was a bag of bones, Dennis liked to eat, and his bedsheets were always full of crumbs and discarded sandwich crusts and spilt things. Despite being covered in bits of food and drink most of the time, Dennis routinely refused the offer of a shower and didn't seem too concerned with his personal hygiene. Since he was the one busy dying, it seemed reasonable to let it slide.

He couldn't get up to use the toilet because he was too weak, so he had several pee bottles nestled in holsters that clipped on to the railing around his bed. He always positioned them right next to his food and beverages, and beside an ever-present box of tissues. There was an ongoing battle of wills over the positioning of the bottles. The nurses continually moved them away from his food supplies for hygiene reasons, and Dennis always moved them straight back, but *that* wasn't even the gross part. Hospital urinal bottles are made of an almost transparent plastic, and the wee in them is most often shades of yellow and amber, and sometimes tinted pink to bright red if there is some degree of bleeding present. Most of the patients were on fluid balance charts where we recorded the volume, colour and pH of the urine output, which gave an indication of hydration status. Dennis's bottles were unique. They were cloudy and stuffed with gummed up tissues because he *wanked* into them. And although it was difficult to begrudge a dying man his only remaining pleasure in life, I still managed it.

Luckily for me, I'd had so many noisy-bar-shouted conversations the night before my day with Dennis that I'd lost my voice by lunchtime, which made me sound as ill as I felt, and I was so pale and wretched looking that my boss believed I was genuinely sick and told me to go home. She didn't have to say it twice. It was a stay of execution, and I have never felt so relieved in my life, except for one time when I really needed to pee and had to wait for two hours to find a bathroom. This was a very close second.

When Dennis died two weeks later, it was undignified to the very end. A lot of patients who are terminally ill have a 'Not For Resuscitation' (NFR) order in place, so that when they die, no active or invasive resuscitation measures, like chest compressions or intubation, are carried out. A relatively dignified death was sometimes the only bright spot left for patients on a long, dark journey of illness and harsh treatments. Dennis had refused to discuss such an order with the doctors or his next of kin – his 85-year-old mother – so when he stopped breathing and his heart finally gave out, we were legally obliged to try to bring him back.

A nurse went to check that Dennis had taken all his Oxycontin tablets after dinner – he refused to take his medication under supervision as he was supposed to because he 'didn't appreciate being rushed' – and he was lying in bed, dead-eyed and open-jawed, the painkillers still bunched in the palm of his hand. The nurse hit the red buzzer by Dennis's bed, which let everybody know that someone was dead or heading that way, and which disturbingly had the same chime as the sound for price checks at my local supermarket. Price checks always put the fear of God into me and got my adrenaline racing; grocery shopping could be a fraught experience.

The crash trolley was rushed to Dennis's bedside. I didn't want to be actively involved in the salvage operation, so I grabbed the clipboard and started documenting the event, a compulsory part of every medical emergency, and the only clean, guaranteed body-fluid-free job in the whole mess. Dennis weighed about as much as a bag of sugar by then, and as the first set of compressions was given, the nurse hovering over him felt his brittle bones crack beneath the heel of her hand. She blanched and looked like she was going to be sick, then continued pumping on his chest, grim-faced.

It was futile but we had no choice. Lines were inserted, atropine and other heart-starting drugs were injected, and someone yelled, 'Stand clear! Shocking now!' and his body jolted on the mattress as the defibrillator attempted to blast him back to life.

Still, there was nothing, and as the compressions continued on what was now clearly a corpse, we all exchanged looks and shook our heads, just waiting for the doctor to say when.

Wherever Dennis was now, he was never coming back. I hoped, for his sake, that he had ended up in a non-Asian section of heaven or he was going to make it hell for everybody else, and that kind of afterlife wouldn't be fun for anyone.

Christos

You learnt a lot of skills on the fly in nursing, because there was really no other way to learn some things, like taking blood from a patient's arm, or giving PR medications, which stands for '*per rectum*', and is exactly what you think it is and just as awful as you would expect. When a transplant patient spiked a temperature, the source of infection had to be tracked down as quickly as possible, due to that whole hanging-on-to-life-by-a-thread thing, so the ability to take blood samples peripherally, whether from an arm, a foot or a hand, as part of a comprehensive septic screen, was essential. When the doctors knew what kind of bugs they were dealing with, they could construct the most effective pharmaceutical regime for killing them. It was a war and, to help win the war, I was packed off to the Outpatients Department, where people presented for blood collections, to spend a couple of hours with a phlebotomist and learn their craft.

An experienced bloodsucker showed me what to do with the tourniquet, how to clip it on and when to let it go, and how to anchor the syringe so I didn't yank it around while it was lodged in some poor bastard's arm and spray the room with blood. After a little coaching, I was let loose on the patients. I had to perform *ten* successful venipunctures before I would be considered qualified to separate patients from their precious plasma.

The first couple of blood draws were nervously conducted. I missed a vein, or it rolled, and I took no pleasure in having to stab people repeatedly, but I gradually got the hang of it. Some people had really shitty veins that stopped flowing with only a millimetre of blood in the chamber, but I generally began to feel more confident. Until patient number eight turned up, and he *hiccuped*.

'You have the hiccups?' I asked, slightly startled.

'Yeah, that's what the bloods are for. I've had them for three weeks.' *Hic.*

I stared at him. 'No way,' I said. 'You're kidding me.'

The guy shook his head. 'No, really!' he said, hiccuping again. 'It's true!'

'You've had the hiccups for *three weeks*? Non-stop?' I was incredulous.

He nodded. 'Yep.'

'How do you *sleep*? That must be driving you crazy!'

'Yeah, it (*hic*) is.'

'Wow,' I said. 'Well, I'm sorry for your trouble.'

But I was even sorrier for myself, because he still needed bloods taken, and the constant jolting made an already difficult task nigh on fucking impossible. I swear, someone somewhere was laughing at me. My confidence took a battering, and so did the poor arm of my unfortunate friend.

Christos, who preferred to be called Chris, had just turned 39 when I met him on his first day in hospital. I gave him the inaugural tour of the ward, since it was going to become his whole world for the best part of the next year, and showed him to his room. His eyes darted around nervously as he took in the other patients, who were bald, or wispy and almost bald, and at various junctures of the spectrum between unwell and extremely unwell. Chris was worried about much more than his hair falling out, but since it was the one fear he freely admitted to, we shaved his head on the first night and got it out of the way; it was the Bruce Willis approach to balding. Fortunately, Chris had a handsome skull and shaving his head looked okay. Some people looked like coneheads or giant eggs. It must have sucked extra hard for those people to have cancer. Nobody could tell you had an unfortunately-shaped cranium when you grew hair all over it, but there was nowhere to hide when you were chemo-bald.

Chris's wife, Lisa, was upbeat and positive about everything, including Chris being HIV positive. She was convinced that he was going to beat the considerable odds and get to see their kids grow up. Charlie was three years old, Sophie was one and, miraculously, Lisa and the children were negative. Lisa was Chris's second wife. He had lived in Vietnam with his first wife for five years, until she abruptly abandoned him, leaving him with mammoth credit card debt and HIV among other things. He had no idea she was a carrier, and didn't find out until he went for a routine medical when he returned to Australia. He had been feeling quite fatigued, assumed it was stress induced and then discovered that he was HIV positive and probably had been for several years.

Still reeling from the diagnosis, he had met Lisa, and they were married five months later since time was of the essence. Now Chris had the family he had always wanted, but he was sick and only going to get sicker. Lisa was buoyant and enthusiastic, some might say delusional, and pinned affirmations all around the room where Chris could see them because she believed the power of positive thinking was going to save him if modern medicine couldn't, and everybody hoped he would prove her right.

Chris was hyper-vigilant about transmission.

'I'm HIV positive, please be very careful,' he would warn anyone who came near him with a syringe. When I was taking blood from his arm, or removing a needle from his skin after an injection, I was acutely aware of the risk if I slipped up and managed to stab myself. I had stuck myself once before with another patient's insulin needle, without consequences, but if I pierced the plastic skin of my glove now, my life could implode just like his had. I made sure I really concentrated on what I was doing, especially on night duty when my motor skills were dumbed down by fatigue, because I didn't want to end up like Chris. He was in hospital for weeks on end, chained to an I-Med pump, poked and prodded a million times, and asked to piss in a bottle and shit into a bowl. Nothing was sacred in hospital, especially not when you had cancer. Privacy did not exist. People were always at you, asking you what you had had to eat or drink and if you had moved your bowels and if you were in pain, but never if you had a sore head from the endless questioning and scrutiny and examination. I guess there was no need to ask; the answer would always have been a resounding *yes*.

The antiretroviral medications and blood transfusions helped keep Chris alive, but the steroids kept him awake. When I checked on him on night duty, he was often staring out the window at the lit-up grey concrete buildings and stewing over everything. He talked about it sometimes, but there wasn't much I could say. His situation sucked, no doubt about it. He was understandably bitter that his life had come to this at 39, and angry that he had been cheated out of a future that everybody takes for granted. The sense that it could have been avoided somehow – if he hadn't met his first wife, had gone to Bali on holiday instead of Vietnam – permeated everything. At night, with no distractions to break the spell, he fixated on all the useless 'if onlys'. And now he had a secondary disease, lymphoma, and that meant he had officially crossed over from HIV to AIDS and his immune system was stuffed. His elderly parents, who visited every day, didn't know about the HIV. Cancer was something they could get their heads around and pray to God for, and apparently AIDS wasn't.

The haematologists fed him hope, because that was their

major commodity. If he could just get through this next round of chemotherapy, then *maybe* he could go on to a bone marrow transplant . . . That baby carrot was the only light in an ink-black tunnel, the only incentive on offer, and it was absurd. 'Why do they put nails in coffins?' the joke went. 'To keep the haematologists out.' They would try anything, and when you had nothing to lose, that was something, at least. The doctors pulled out all the stops and kept going until the patient said when, or until they were too unwell to say anything at all.

Over the course of his illness's progression, Chris began to look like one of those nodding dogs in the back of a car. His neck was a stick, his Adam's apple protruding painfully from his neck. He said that every part of his body ached. One time I caught him swigging greedily from a bottle of liquid morphine in his room, oblivious to the risk of over-dosing, as he tried to blot out the pain.

'Please don't tell anyone!' he pleaded. 'They'll take it away from me!'

And as much as I didn't want to, I had to. He was going to kill himself with that shit, without even meaning to, and he didn't need any help in that department.

One of the things Chris got to experience when his blood test results came back looking really messed up was a 'bone marrow aspirate'. It didn't even *sound* nice. Local anaesthetic was pricked into his back and then a large nee-dle was inserted into his sufficiently numbed spine. Chris couldn't feel it, but still had to be present for it, conscious, with his back bent over a table or some other stable surface so the doctor could find exactly the right spot. Each attempt to extract cerebrospinal fluid was called 'a pass'.

So, the first pass failed. There was no clear fluid being released. The doctor went in for a second pass and again, nothing. Eventually, with the doctor growing ever more frustrated, starting to sweat and beginning to doubt her ability, a few drops appeared in the hollow tube like honey and were sent to pathology for review. If eyes were the windows to your soul, then cerebrospinal fluid, or CSF, was a window to your actual core. If the chemotherapy and all the drugs had worked, Chris's CSF would show it. And if they hadn't, it would show that, too.

Three weeks after his 40th birthday, Christos started rambling and talking nonsense at nine pm. Lisa was worried. His oxygen levels were dropping slightly, so we stuck green plastic prongs up his nose and started him on two litres of oxygen. He asked me what my name was. I told him.

He said, 'I'm forgetting things.'

His oxygen levels dropped again and his breathing began to pick up pace and became slightly shallow. We turned the oxygen up again. It climbed, four litres, six litres, ten litres, and Chris became confused and agitated. Lisa started to cry and he just looked through her, not comprehending anything. When his parents arrived, he didn't recognise them.

The doctor turned up to review Chris, and immediately called in the consultant, who came to the ward at two in the morning. He examined Chris, his most recent blood results, and told us to start a subcutaneous syringe driver, a little box of morphine that delivered continuous pain relief via a butterfly needle that was embedded in the subcutaneous tissue, just beyond the skin. It marked the beginning of the end. The consultant spoke to the family and told them it was unlikely Chris was going to make it through the night. Nobody wanted to believe it. They huddled around him, in shock, crying. That morning he had been pale and tired and a little less talkative than usual, but he was still there, still Chris, and now he was vanishing.

Chris's eyes had been open and empty and not focussed on anything for the last few hours, but now they were closed. He hadn't peed in hours, his feet and hands were cold to the touch because his circulation was shutting down.

I stayed on the periphery of the room, not wanting to intrude, and there was nothing to do but wait, anyway. Emma, the nurse I was working with, and I took it in turns to check on him, hovering by the door. It felt like the night was never going to end, but then the sun started to rise, red in the distance, and Chris stopped breathing.

Lisa screamed, 'Help! Come quickly!'

Chris was wearing a re-breather mask, an oxygen mask with another bag attached, and both of them were still.

Lisa screamed at him, 'Breathe, Chris! Breathe!' and thumped on his chest, compelling him to live. I felt for the carotid pulse in his neck, and it faded beneath my fingertips, then I pressed a stethoscope to his heart and listened.

There was only silence in my ears, and I was going to have to tell them. I felt like an actor saying the words, but the effect they had was painfully real.

'I'm sorry, but I think he's gone.' And everybody broke down, screaming and crying, and I had to leave the room. It was unbearable.

After a few minutes of heartbroken wailing, the noise began to subside and I stepped quietly back into the room to turn the oxygen off and take the mask off his face so they could see him properly.

His 70-year-old mother hit me in the chest and shoved me. 'Get away from him! Get away!'

I understood, but I was upset too, and so fucking tired on top of everything else. I started to choke up. When I walked out, Emma saw I was upset and told me to take a break. She phoned the doctor on call and started getting the paperwork in order.

I went to the staffroom, made myself a cup of tea and tried not to lose it. After the slow decline of the last year, Chris's exit had felt so rushed. It always felt sudden when somebody you had seen most days for 12 months died, and I had liked Chris a lot, too. Patients weren't friends, exactly, but in some ways, friendship wasn't a strong enough word to describe it. There really wasn't a name for what we were to each other.

A lot of people passed away as the sun came up. It was like a signal, or a kiss. This day was not for you, but you left this planet, this plane, at its most beautiful. The world was sending you off with gentle fanfare, in a bright pink-and-orange-hued dawn.

The Ancient Miner

The first indication that this particular shift was going to suck more dick than ten brothels was when I discovered that I had been partnered with an agency nurse. Three people had called in sick for the afternoon and none of the regular staff were willing to work any overtime so one of the nursing temp agencies had been contacted, and a body sent. Her name was Harriet, and she was mine for the next eight hours. She walked up to the nurse's station at the beginning of the shift and I wished I'd had the foresight to call in sick myself.

Harriet was about five foot tall and 50-something with a crew cut and the kind of huge owlish glasses last seen on Sally Jessy Raphael. She also had a customised tool belt buckled around her waist with an array of nursing accoutrements – tweezers, forceps, and several pairs of scissors – that clinked and chimed like Christmas bells every time she moved. The fluorescent pink stethoscope wrapped around her neck had several labels affixed at various intervals along it, which stated, 'PROPERTY OF HARRIET JONES, REGISTERED NURSE,' in case anybody got crazy and considered using it. But the pièce de résistance was the halogen headlamp strapped to her forehead, which made her look like a Dalek. Oh, and it also made her look *fucking ridiculous*. I was going to have to bite my tongue for eight hours, seven and a half if I got away from her at dinner time.

'Hi, I'm Kristy,' I introduced myself, trying to be as friendly and welcoming as possible, overcompensating for the evil thoughts in my head. 'You'll be working with me today.'

'Harriet Jones, RN,' she replied mechanically, without so much as a hint of a smile. 'I take my dinner break at eighteen hundred hours.'

'Oh . . . Okay, sure.'

Harriet tilted her head and looked up, testing her headlamp on the ceiling by flicking it on and off twice, then turned her gaze back to me, still unsmiling. Harriet looked like she had a lot of cats, and the traits of several mental illnesses.

There never seemed to be a middle ground with an agency nurse. They were either a godsend, or a giant albatross around your neck. Ostensibly, you had someone to do half the work, but in reality you spent half the shift explaining how to *do* that half of the work, which cut into the available time by a quarter, and often a third, depending on the temperament and level of expertise of your substitute nurse. By the time you had explained how to do something, you could have done it yourself at least twice. Often you *would* just do it yourself, and an agency nurse could have a pretty sweet shift doing simple tasks like observations and emptying bedpans and staying out of my way, for 50 bucks an hour.

Harriet, the Ancient Miner, had temped in my ward before, so she didn't need a guided tour, or to be shown where the drugs were kept or where the pan room was. She went to check on the eight patients we had been allocated and I started writing up our work schedule, which meant sifting through all the medication charts and recording fluid rates and times that antibiotics and other drugs were due. I was halfway through when Harriet approached.

'Is the patient in Room 21 meant to be dead?' she asked me.

I looked up from my paperwork. 'Sorry?'

'The patient in *Room 21*,' she said, like I was deaf or retarded. 'Is he *meant to be dead*?'

I stared at her for a few seconds, pleasantly surprised that she had enough of a sense of humour to make a joke, and then suddenly realised that she didn't. OHMYGOD.

I jumped up and ran into Room 21, and could hear Harriet lumbering after me, tinkling like the tooth fairy with a bag full of coins.

The patient in Room 21 wasn't just dead, he was cold to the touch. He appeared to have left the building some time ago.

'Shit, shit, *shit*!' I said, as I felt for a non-existent carotid pulse, then hit the emergency buzzer on the wall.

Harriet snapped on a pair of gloves and held the patient's left eye open with one hand, flicked on her headlamp with the other and moved her head from side to side, scanning for signs of life.

A bad day at work in nursing was not like when other people had a bad day at work. It's true that nobody had stolen my yoghurt from the staffroom fridge when I had *specifically* put my name on it, and nobody had forgotten to give me a really important fax about something really important, but trying to fit an inflexible body into a bag, and telling someone you're very sorry but their husband has 'gone' was no picnic either.

If you were in the business of looking after really sick people, then you knew that you were going to lose a few from time to time, but you could never be sure exactly when, and sometimes they took everybody by surprise. I was a big fan of the tentative patient-related enquiry from a fellow nurse, which was actually an ultra-loaded question. The casual delivery was somewhat disarming, like a bomb disposal expert asking, 'So, what happens if you *accidentally* cut the red wire?' prior to them exploding into stew.

At two thirty in the morning I sat at the nurses' station labelling my blood tubes for our early morning collection, while Erin, the Clinical Nurse in charge of the shift, updated her handover notes. The next flurry of ward activity was due to begin at 3.30 and wouldn't stop until our shift ended at seven.

'Hey, is Bed 2 for resus?' a nurse named Matthew coolly asked as he emerged from Bed 2's single room. When a patient was NFR it was marked on the handover sheet in big, bold capital letters. The patient in Bed 2 was clearly *not* marked NFR. Therefore, he was most definitely FR: *For* Resuscitation.

'Yeah, why?' Erin replied distractedly, after a quick glance at the handover sheet.

'Oh, well, resus for Bed 2, then. He's dead.'

As the emergency alarms went off, rudely waking every person in the building who *was* alive, a collective 'Ah, *great!*' was muttered by all the nurses. I groaned and headed for the dead guy. It was sad, and it was also *really* inconvenient. 'Resus' or a 'medical emergency' meant that the carefully orchestrated work plan for the shift was now shot to shit. Half the nurses on the ward were going to be bagging and delivering vigorous chest compressions and oxygen to a deceased patient for the foreseeable future, and then there was all the accompanying paperwork to complete afterwards. Clearly, the outcome for the poor guy who had died was much worse, but an arrest smack-bang in the middle of a night shift was the crappiest timing imaginable. The automatic adrenaline surge dissipated after an hour or so of frantic activity, and was replaced by a thundering crash. Already struggling to stay awake as you defied nature's circadian rhythm, the inescapable, extreme fatigue was a double helping of shit with an extra serving of shit on the side, and no amount of coffee made a dent in it. Brain and body spent, and with several hours of work to go, and eight other patients requiring their second, fourth, sixth and eighth hourly drugs to be given on time, you just staggered on to the finish line in excruciatingly painful slow motion.

★

Washing the body is part of the etiquette of patient care – care all the way to the end of the line. The first body I had to wash was a woman who had died of liver failure, and she had such severe jaundice when she passed away that she was almost luminous. Her skin was a sickly, bright yellow, the result of her body stockpiling bilirubin.

After her family had some time alone to say goodbye, a couple of us went into her room with warm soapy water, fresh linen and towels. Her skin was warm and we talked to her like she was still there, because even if her vital signs weren't, she *was* still there. I thought it would feel different to touch a dead person, but it didn't really. The only difference was that she felt heavier because all her muscles had relaxed; it would be some time before the inevitable arrival of rigor mortis. It was quite a messy exercise, but we cleaned her up and spoke to her gently as we worked.

We placed a fresh sheet over her and she lay in bed, arms by her side and looking asleep for all intents and purposes, except for the absolute stillness. Looking after dead people was no different to looking after the living and breathing. It all came back to treating others the way you would like to be treated, and the way you would want your family and friends to be treated. And I didn't want there to be any *Weekend At Bernie's* waterskiing-type nonsense going down when I died.

Genevieve

Genevieve had been having a lot of chemotherapy and her guts knew all about it. Nausea, vomiting and diarrhoea had been the status quo for the last month, and they showed no sign of abating. Genny had non-Hodgkin's lymphoma, yet another variation in an apparently endless stream of blood cancers, and unfortunately hers was the aggressive kind, so she had been bombarded with chemotherapy straight off the bat. The idea was to take the lymphoma out before it took *her* out, and there wasn't much time to act.

Genny had lost a lot of weight since the onset of her chemotherapy regime and, as she was quite thin to begin with, she was now a tiny, emaciated sparrow of a woman. On the rare occasion she managed to keep her food down, it seemed to pass through her almost intact, barely altered by the process of digestion, and I knew this because I frequently had to empty her bedpans. A lot of the time it was hard to tell if it was 'before' or 'after' hospital food just by looking at it, and it was only the fact that it was sitting at the bottom of a bedpan that let you know for sure. Yes, the world of ward nursing was truly a glamorous one. Most days I had major career envy when I saw the ward receptionist answering the phone and tapping away on her keyboard. She was so close to the unpleasantness, and yet, she was so far away.

Genevieve's buzzer had just gone off, so I stuck my head in the door, hesitantly, because her room was pretty much the worst-smelling place on the ward, and that was no small achievement in the often odious Bone Marrow stink pit. Her room didn't smell like grim death in the way that graft-versus-host disease disintegration did, but it was still an oppressive, stomach-turning environment. Whenever Genny was in the bathroom, as she was at least 20 times a day, we discreetly sprayed her room with deodoriser to make it more bearable for our frequent drug dispensing and observational visits. Genny herself seemed to be immune to the stench. It was either Dalai Lama-type acceptance or her sense of smell had been wiped out, a la Hiroshima, with the unceasing production of gastrointestinal 'dirty bombs'.

On this occasion, Genny was sitting up in bed with a pained expression on her face, grimacing and resting on her knuckles in order to lift her arse up off the mattress and minimise the pressure caused by sitting.

'What's up, Genny?' I asked her.

'My bum's really sore,' she said, wincing. 'Can you have a look at it for me?'

Call it intuition, or self-preservation, or chickenshit-tery, but I had a hunch that I shouldn't go in there alone. I needed to call for back-up.

'Yeah, sure, Genny. Just give me a second, I'll be right back,' I replied.

I found my nurse buddy, Sarah, and asked her to come with me to examine Genny's arse. She kindly agreed to be my wingman.

We went back into Genny's room, pulled the curtain closed around her bed for privacy and asked her to lower the adult nappy she was wearing. When she did, Sarah and I both gasped in horror.

'Do I need some Rectinol cream or something?' Genny asked, sounding pained.

'Um, no, I think you need something a bit stronger than that,' Sarah said calmly, not wanting to alarm her, because Genevieve's rectum had prolapsed after all the stress and strain of continuous diarrhoea and the inside of her arse was now on the outside, red raw and hanging out like a donut made of mincemeat. It was *horrific*. I would never be able to look at trays of hamburger mince in the supermarket again without experiencing a mild post-traumatic flashback.

'Okay, Genny, just hop back into bed and try to relax,' Sarah said in the most casual tone of voice she could muster in the circumstances, 'and we'll get the doctor to come and take a look at you.'

'Alright.' Genny grimaced, easing herself gently back down on to the mattress and then carefully rolling over on to her side.

Sarah and I stepped outside Genny's room and closed the door behind us. Sarah looked completely stunned and I burst out laughing. My reaction to shock was always hysterical laughter, and it could be an awkward thing, like the time a cupboard had toppled over on to my younger sister. She lay spreadeagled on the ground, pinned to the floor by a large item of furniture like she was a piece of paper thumbtacked to a memo board. I had lost it laughing and she had never forgiven me for it, which was understandable because it *did* seem like a jerk move on my part, but it was actually an involuntary nervous system response, rather than malicious enjoyment. *I* knew where my uncontrollable giggling was coming from, and that it didn't originate from a place of evil, but that didn't make it any easier to explain to other people, and especially not when I happened to be laughing my head off in a cancer ward because someone's bum had just fallen out.

Sarah went to tell the nurse in charge of the shift about the prolapse and I called the doctor. I tried to calm down and control myself so I could tell him what had happened without dissolving into continued fits of inappropriate laughter.

'Oh my god! I'll be right there!' he said, panicked, and he was on the ward within two minutes, examining her. He emerged from Genny's room looking pale and very worried. He was a young doctor, and it was obviously his first time at the prolapse rodeo, too.

I was still giggling, and now Sarah was too, and the doctor looked at us, bewildered and appalled.

'She could *die* from this, you know!' he said, and we both wanted to stop laughing but it had gone too far. We were helpless. The harder we tried, the worse it became. My stomach muscles were *aching*.

'I know,' I told him. 'I'm not laughing because it's funny . . .' But that just made us laugh even more and I had to go to the bathroom and splash cold water on my face to get a grip while Sarah started drawing up morphine, her shoulders still subtly shaking.

A prolapsed rectum was awful, and the treatment for it was too, so it was a lose/lose situation for everybody involved. The 'cure' involved administering a significant amount of morphine or other hardcore analgesia to the patient, before gently pushing what had fallen out back in. And unfortunately, if it had weakened and fallen out once, it tended to keep happening. Genevieve spent the next week sitting on the toilet having her rectum turn suddenly concave, followed by a morphine chaser and a nurse *literally* giving her a hand.

Nursing is great at putting life in perspective and making you grateful for the obvious things, like being cancer free, and the not-so-obvious things it would usually never occur to me to be thankful for, like possession of sphincter muscle tone and one's ability to take a dump without having one's arse turn inside out. I spent a lot of time saying silent thank yous to the powers that be for not giving me leukaemia or lymphoma, or a prolapsed rectum. And on top of that, I gave thanks for not being allocated the patients at Genevieve's end of the ward while her internal architecture continued to collapse like a house of cards.

Poor Genevieve eventually recovered. The diarrhoea slowed, then stopped, and her bowel finally got a chance to stay put. She was going to need surgery to fix the prolapse in the future, if the lymphoma and its aftermath didn't get to her first, but she was safe for the moment. She finally left the ward after many long months, as slight as a whisper but still largely intact, and returned home with boxes and bags of medication that would hopefully keep her well. Before she departed she gave a thank you card to the ward that said, among other things, *Thanks for looking after me and my arse.*

When it came to invasive, unpleasant treatment options, the Oncology and Bone Marrow Unit represented a triple threat, because we had chemotherapy and bone marrow transplants and all that they entailed, but we *also* had a special corner of the ward reserved for brachytherapy, or internal radiotherapy, and radioactive 'swallows'.

Imagine this scenario, if you will.

'You've got cancer.' Not what you want to hear.

'You've got cancer of the cervix.' Even less so.

'And the way we treat cervical cancer is to insert rods into your vagina and pulse them with radiation hourly for 72 hours.' And I'm *out*.

But wait, there's more!

'You'll have a catheter inserted into your bladder so you can urinate freely into a bag, since you won't be able to get up to go to the bathroom because the rods will be *surgically attached* to your lady bits. We'll give you a couple of enemas before you get to theatre to have the rods placed, so that you don't have to move your bowels, because we *really* don't want you to shit the bed and interfere with the radiation, although that doesn't always go to plan, unfortunately . . . Basically, you'll be stuck in a bed with metal rods up your twat, unable to move and being zapped with radiation every hour, and eating and sleeping in a position that is half sitting up and half lying down for three whole days. If you're agreeable to it, the nurses can give you a fairly half-arsed sponge bath, which will probably just make you feel damp and sticky and less clean than you did before. Also, because radiation is so dangerous, there are alarms attached to the machine and, if the rods move *at all*, there will be a godawful blaring noise to alert the medical staff. If you're fortunate enough to have fallen asleep in the first place, despite the extreme and prolonged discomfort of your prone position, well, that will wake you up rather abruptly, and we're very sorry about that but it's a significant safety concern, as I'm sure you can appreciate . . . Oh, and I should also mention that red flashing lights will be going off at the same time, so you'll kind of feel like you're at a really terrible nightclub without any drugs, but don't worry! All the commotion will wake up everybody else in the ward, too, especially if the alarm goes off at four in the morning as so frequently happens, but at least then you won't feel so alone, there in your single bed in your isolated room. And you thought *cancer* was bad! It's only the beginning . . .'

Radioactive iodine swallows for thyroid cancer were another treatment option offered and, on paper, it seemed very simple. The patient was given a capsule containing radioactive iodine, which was absorbed by the thyroid gland and began obliterating cancerous cells. Any left-over radiation *not* taken up by the thyroid was washed out in body waste over a three-day period, thanks to a high-fibre diet and several litres of liquids. As far as nurse and patient involvement went, there wasn't really supposed to be any. The patients were locked away in their secure, lead-lined rooms and the only interaction was supposed to be when the nurses did a drop-and-run mission delivering the patients their meals and simultaneously removing the double-knotted bags of rubbish from their rooms. We had to scan the discarded bags with a Geiger counter to see if they were at levels safe enough to go straight into the general waste or if they needed to be locked away in the 'hot box' and disposed of by a physicist, and we all wore little individual Geiger counters to measure our personal radiation exposure. If anybody's level came back elevated, they were exempt from working in the radiation suite for a few months. For the most part, the system worked perfectly well, although one notable exception rushes to mind. As fuckups went, it was *big*.

A Russian gentleman with thyroid cancer turned up for a routine iodine swallow. He was schizophrenic, from an actively non-English-speaking background and, unbe-known to anyone, had critically low sodium levels because his blood results were helpfully returned *after* he had been given his capsule. This meant that instead of the radia-tion being eliminated as he consumed his litres of fluid, as planned, his body held on to every drop of hydration for dear life, and hence every particle of radiation. He rapidly swelled up into an overloaded radioactive balloon as his sodium levels continued to plummet.

'Oh, *shit*,' the nurse in charge said, and oh shit was right. Before long, he was confused and standing in the doorway of his room, grinning madly and buck naked except for a woollen beanie perched on his head. Why his head felt cold when the rest of him seemed perfectly content nude at room temperature was a mystery, but we couldn't ask him about it because when we called the phone in his room, he just stared at it. And when he *did* finally pick it up – after the tenth call – he spoke Russian into the wrong end of the receiver.

We observed him via the closed-circuit television system and watched as he grew fatter and rounder until he looked like Augustus Gloop. His sodium levels needed to be boosted urgently and he was too bloated and radioactive for a doctor to put an IV line in him and deliver saline directly, so we concocted a foul potion of salt sachets and lemon cordial and then took it in turns to spend a maximum of 20 seconds forcing him to drink it. Fifteen minutes before the end of my 12-hour shift, it was my turn to go in again.

'You need to drink this,' I told him, and he looked at me vacantly. I put the cup to his lips and poured some of the drink into his mouth, with an exaggerated mime of swallowing to show him what to do with it.

'Swallow! Swallow!' I yelled, but he just grinned at me stupidly. And then two thin trickles of blood suddenly ran down from both corners of his mouth and, between the blood and the grinning, he looked like a nightmarishly grotesque clown. His tongue almost bitten in half, he proceeded to have a full-blown seizure and *then* stopped breathing. I told you it was a big fuckup.

I swore my head off, hit the emergency alarm button on the wall, and the nurses who had been watching the slow-motion horror show on the closed-circuit television outside burst into the room to help. With superhuman, adrenaline-charged power, we rolled the patient over on to his side, scooped the radioactive blood out of his mouth, and got him breathing again while the alarms sounded like a German air raid was imminent. *Fifteen more minutes and I would have been in the clear,* I thought to myself, but typically, this epic shitstorm had impeccable timing.

At the end of the shift, the nurses involved in the calamitous resuscitation effort were corralled into the physicist's office to have thyroid scans and our radiation levels checked after prolonged exposure at close proximity.

I wasn't very optimistic about an accurate reading, especially when the physicist muttered vaguely, 'Um, well, I *think* this is how the machine works. I've never had to use it before . . .'

We were all given a clean bill of health, for what it was worth, and very shortly after this incident, I thought, *Hey, FUCK THIS!* and began making enquiries about a radiation- and chemotherapy-free nursing position. It was one thing to be dissatisfied with my job, and quite another to be nuked while doing it.

Princess

I had hated my third-year placement in the Neurology and Stroke Unit so much that when I heard there had been an outbreak of gastroenteritis on the ward, I pretended I had it, too, so I wouldn't have to go in. I *wanted* gastro if it meant any kind of reprieve from a place where patients had to be winched on industrial hoists just to have a shower, or fed through a tube, or repositioned every two hours in a bed they would be stuck in until they passed away, or shuttled out to a nursing home, only to die there instead. Those patients had a quality of life, or lack thereof, that made death seem merciful, and their survival of a cerebro-vascular accident nothing less than tragic. Depending on the type of stroke they had suffered, which functions of the brain had been affected and to what degree, some patients didn't exhibit marked physical injury, but got lost just walking to the toilet, or had their speech reduced to 'word salad', where coherent thoughts were expressed as a confused jumble.

Strokes changed people's personalities, too. They were internal seismic shifts, rupturing the core of an individual until there was no longer any correlation between the person they had been before the stroke and the person they were afterwards, except for the body that contained them. It was incredibly depressing, and definitely not the sort of work I could handle, but thankfully it was a good fit for some people. When I said that I had applied for a job in Oncology and Bone Marrow Transplant, all the Stroke nurses screwed their faces up and said, '*Eww!* Why would you want to work *there*?' Which was exactly what the Oncology nurses said when I told them I had been on a placement in the Stroke Ward for three months.

And it was what *everybody* said when I told them that I was going to work in Drug and Alcohol Detoxification.

Bums, lawyers, housewives, architects – they all ended up in Detox eventually, often with nothing much in common except lives turning to shit in a terrific hurry.

After the many sad moments of the Bone Marrow Transplant Unit, I was initially buoyed by the seeming simplicity of Detox. There were no multi-channel I-Med machines or complicated medication regimes to manage, no cytotoxic materials to be exposed to, and no chance of my being irradiated in the course of my day and possibly having children with tails and webbed feet. The fact that there was one oxygen cylinder for the whole ward, instead of one within arm's reach of each extremely ill patient, was refreshing, as was the fact that the resuscitation trolley was kept in a locked cupboard because it was hardly ever used. I was in a clinically foreign world, but I felt much more at home than I ever had in the Transplant Unit. Depending on the patients, the ward could be pleasant and settled, or completely mental and a bit scary, but it was rarely dull. Detox was an environment in flux. One minute the place was empty and you were knocking around empty corridors, the next minute it was pure chaos, but I actually enjoyed going to work, and didn't feel like killing myself on the last day of holidays at the thought of going back there. I rode that giddy wave for about a year, before it became a job like any other and the tail-end of holidays became just as big a downer as it had always been.

Becoming accustomed to people blatantly lying to your face, and doing it so well that you really couldn't tell, was one of the major adjustments I had to make in Detox. I felt like the most naïve person on the planet and wondered how I had ever believed a word *anyone* said to me, because it soon felt like the whole world was a dirty liar. Playing dumb was the main ploy. And a lot of the patients weren't playing, they were dumb as lint, but they had such finely honed rat cunning that the most street-hardened rat would have felt bad about themselves in comparison.

Our ward was a non-smoking area, like every other part of the hospital, but that didn't stop patients from smoking, and part of our duty of care was to ensure that they weren't endangering themselves or others by sparking up in the toilets or the bathrooms and setting themselves on fire. I felt like a high school teacher, or the piss-weak police, hunting down the renegades who lined the bathroom doors with damp towels to trap the smoke, but neglected to realise that the closed ventilation system just pumped it through the rest of the ward. The source was usually easy enough to locate, but that didn't stop people from lying about it.

'Have you been smoking?' I asked one patient.

'No,' he said, wide-eyed and innocent, as a wisp of smoke snaked out of his mouth.

Then a phone buzzed, very nearby. Mobile phones were also forbidden on the ward, and confiscated upon admission.

'Do you have a mobile phone?'

'No.' He looked around, feigning bewilderment, like the noise was coming from some mystifying parallel dimension, and not his obviously vibrating pocket.

'I think that's your phone . . .'

'Oh, *that* phone . . . Oh, *yeah*! Sorry, I forgot that was there!'

Now that he had been caught smoking *and* with a mobile phone on his person, he was asked to leave the ward. He had twice broken the behavioural contract he had signed on admission and there was a strict 'one strike and you're out' policy, which was the ward's only saving grace. He protested that it was totally unfair and how he thought nurses were supposed to *care* about people. He said that by kicking him out we were *forcing* him to go out and use drugs again, and he hoped we could live with that knowledge. And then he pulled another mobile phone out of his sock and called a mate to organise a lift home.

I met Princess in my first few weeks on the Detox ward, when I was feeling pretty fresh. He had come into Detox to get off heroin and I had come to get off the Bone Marrow death ship.

Princess, as the moniker suggests, was a royal pain in the arse. I felt quite sorry for him because he was so obviously out of his depth, but that didn't stop him getting on my nerves, or on everybody else's, from the moment he arrived.

Despite a complete absence of any obvious opiate withdrawal symptoms, like constant yawning, gut cramps, a runny nose or watery eyes, Princess was adamant that he was suffering beyond reason and filled out his 'Opiate Withdrawal Scale' accordingly. Each symptom was to be scored on a scale from 0–3 in degree of severity, with '0' being nil and '3' being 'severe'. Princess scored each of his symptoms '5+', which was a sure-fire way of pissing off the nurses, and made the withdrawal scale as redundant as a crossword in terms of therapeutic benefit.

To compound the irritation, Princess also made constant requests for extra medication, a private room, softer blankets and a better mattress. He was shit out of luck on all fronts, and having been on the ward for less than an hour, was not endearing himself to anyone, least of all the other patients, who thought he was a pussy, which was only fair since he looked down on them as street scum. Not even the great equaliser of opiate addiction could level the playing field between the haves and have-nots, and Princess was still firmly ensconced in the 'have' section of society. He hadn't even been to jail. *Yet.*

Princess had been found in his car by the police, on the nod with drugs and a syringe in his lap, and because his keys were in the ignition he was charged with dangerous operation of a motor vehicle as well as other offences. With his day in court coming up, and Princess's wealthy parents finally tired of bankrolling his numerous failed attempts at private detox and rehabilitation, his options were to go cold turkey, which Princess didn't really have the gonads for, or to slum it in a public hospital for a week on the taxpayers' dime. We might not have been what he was used to, but we still had buprenorphine, an opiate substitute that would make getting straight much more tolerable, in theory at least.

The main problem Princess had with Detox was the lack of heroin. We gave him buprenorphine, but it just didn't hit the spot. He had only been on the ward for a few hours when he came out to use the payphone that the patients used to call their friends and family. Or their drug dealers.

I was sitting at the nurses' station reading, while another nurse tidied up the charts. Princess had his back to us and spoke in hushed tones as he organised a deal.

'Yeah, pick me up at the front in half an hour,' he said quietly. He put the phone down and went back to his room then, after a few minutes, came up to the desk. The other nurse and I smiled at each other. We had taken bets about how long Princess would last on the ward, and if he left in the next hour I was going to be five dollars richer. Victory was almost mine. We waited for the line about his grandmother dying, or his house being flooded, or how his girlfriend had spontaneously combusted and was now in a Burns Unit at another hospital.

'Hey,' he said, with a sheepish, almost regretful smile, 'um, I'm really sorry about this, but I have to go.'

'What's up?' I asked.

'Oh, it's not you, guys! The staff here are *great!*' he gushed, overcompensating. 'I just have a few really important things to do at home that I forgot about, and they can't wait.'

'Right,' I said.

'So, thanks for everything, but I'm going to pack my bag,' he said.

'You know that you won't be able to use for about 12 hours because the medication we gave you will throw you into withdrawal, right?' the other nurse casually mentioned, and Princess frowned.

'Sorry?'

'You can't use straightaway, or you'll go into frank withdrawal, the really nasty stuff, so why don't you have a think about it, before you start packing up your things?' he said, and Princess dropped his bundle.

'*I can't do this! It's too hard!*' he whined.

'There's really no way around it.' I shrugged. 'We've given you all the medication we can. You're just going to have to man up.'

Princess shot me a look of disgust, then went to the pay-phone and made another call, this time minus his earlier discretion.

'Yeah, it's me. Forget about the gear, man, I'll call you tomorrow.' He slammed the phone down and went back to his bed to sulk.

Damn. If Princess made it to the morning, *I* was going to be shelling out five bucks, but I was still feeling reasonably confident that I would emerge triumphant.

Princess ended up stomping out at midnight. So nobody won, and especially not him.

The Royal Family, Princess's parents, phoned in the morning for a progress report and were not amused when advised that he was no longer an inpatient on the ward, but the facts were plain: Princess was a voluntary patient; he didn't want to stop using heroin; he left. It sucks, but that was the ugly truth of the matter. He wasn't ready, and he might never be.

The worst part about working in Detox wasn't the patients, not even the ones who punched holes in the walls, or called you a fucking bitch, or threatened to sic their bikie mates the Bandidos on to you. None of that was fun, but what I hated most was answering the phone and having to talk to the patient's family or partner, the worried, frustrated and frightened people who were held hostage because they loved them. They were watching someone slowly drown and desperately throwing them a rope, often only to have it thrown back in their face accompanied by a giant 'FUCK YOU' where a heartfelt 'thank you' should have been.

It was the same story every time, with a few minor alterations.

My boyfriend has a drinking problem . . .

My daughter is taking heroin . . .

My brother is crazy from injecting speed . . . WHAT DO I DO?

The fear and pain was palpable, and hard to stomach. I would spend however long counselling and consoling, reeling off phone numbers and addresses for services and emphasising that the person with the problem was the only one who could fix it.

What I *felt* like saying, but couldn't, was: 'Run away and don't look back. Just *run*.'

The Tampon

I'm pretty sure nobody told me about this sort of thing when I was studying. I could clearly recall lectures about pressure sores, and the different kinds of shock, and learning about potassium and sodium and all the magic invisible processes that made bodies work. I definitely do not remember being warned that some day I would smell something so unholy it would make my eyes water, but even if I had, I would never have believed it could be *that* bad, although now I know better. It can.

After working in Bone Marrow Transplant, I thought I was used to godawful-smelling things. When people developed graft-versus-host disease of the gut, which is basically when the body rejects the transplant and declares war on itself, their insides came out in a foul, continuous purge. If a patient had a gastrointestinal haemorrhage, their bowel motions became tarry and black, also known as 'melena', and it smelt like hell. Chemotherapy-induced diarrhoea was hideous, too, as was shit, generally, and most days there was plenty of it to go around.

I was lulled into a false sense of olfactory security in Detox, because the patients walked around freely and weren't hooked up to IV fluids or machinery, and when a patient threw up and I asked where the sick bags were kept, the other nurses started pulling faces and saying, 'Oh my *god*, she's *throwing up*?' because they didn't normally encounter the more disgusting parts of nursing that were par for the course elsewhere. So I was caught off-guard on a couple of occasions. One of the first instances was when Johnny, a homeless guy, arrived for an alcohol detox. I gave him a little tour of the ward and made a point of showing him where the showers were and got him some hospital pyjamas so he could change out of his filthy clothes. He didn't have shoes – someone had stolen them when he was passed out in a park – and his feet were black and caked in dirt. He smelt like he hadn't bathed in months, if not years, and he hadn't been sober in all that time either, so even a brief walk around the ward tired him out and he asked if he could lie down for a little while. I directed him to his bed and he lay down on top of the covers with his eyes clamped shut and his arms by his side, like a body laid out for viewing.

Five minutes later he was at the nurses' station, holding on to the bench to prevent himself from toppling over backwards. His cerebellum had taken a beating and a half, and he couldn't stand up, or stay up, without support.

'Where's the toilet?' he asked.

'Just down there.' I pointed at the closest lavatory. God, he smelled *terrible*.

He shuffled off down the hall, grabbing on to the hand-rail as he went, but the smell didn't lessen. It lingered and, if anything, the intensity increased. I walked around to the other side of the bench and there it was, waiting.

Ah, shit. 'Code Brown!' I announced, wanting to gag, and the other nurses I was working with groaned. Johnny had lost control of his bowels, leaving a long trail of putrid shit from his bed all the way to the toilet like a Hansel and Gretel trail of breadcrumbs. One of the nurses got a towel, then saw the extent of the mess and fetched the mop and bucket instead. If what was coming out of Johnny was any indication of what was going on inside of him, then he was not a well man.

Tampons come with instructions telling you to change them every three or four hours, and to take them out before you go to bed, and *for crying out loud do not leave them in any longer than that, or you'll get Toxic Shock Syndrome and die.* It wasn't terribly complicated: if you wanted to live a long and healthy life, ladies, you just needed to follow the instructions on the little pamphlet included in each pack and take due care. An additional warning might have been useful for women who drank a shitload of alcohol, however. Perhaps something along the lines of, *If you drink more than 30 standard drinks a day on most days of your life, please consider other, externally placed, sanitary products.*

When one patient finally sobered up enough to realise that she might have left a tampon in *three weeks ago*, it was arranged for her to be reviewed by a doctor as soon as possible, even though she didn't have a temperature or any other symptoms that suggested potential infection or imminent death. She said she felt perfectly fine, actually, but her boyfriend had said that she 'smelt bad . . . down there'.

I shuddered.

The doctor who drew the short straw was a tiny Asian woman with glasses who looked about 16. I handed the patient's notes over to her. She read them, grimaced ever so slightly and then got business-like. She asked for a speculum, forceps, gloves, gown, mask, absorbent sheeting, lubricant and an assistant – which meant *me*, because I happened to be the nurse in front of her at the time. Sometimes you won, like handing your patients over to another nurse to go to lunch and coming back to find that you escaped an episode of double incontinence by mere moments. And sometimes you lost, like being privy to a three-week-old tampon because you were the nurse with the dumb luck to have elected to go on the second lunch break.

Really, how bad can it be? I asked myself. It wasn't as if *I* had to go in there and fish around for a grotty old tampon that may, or may not, be in situ. I was just a bystander, a wingman, and thank god for that. It was times like these I was glad I was an underachiever and not a doctor, and that I had drunk my way to super-average grades, which in turn kept me safely anchored at the nursing end of the medical food chain. *This* was why doctors were paid the big money, and they were more than welcome to it.

'When did you realise that there might be a tampon inside?' the doctor asked as the patient lay back on the bed, drew her knees up and slowly lowered her legs on to the foam mattress. I draped a towel over her groin to protect whatever dignity she had left, and *that's* when the smell hit me in the face, like a runaway garbage truck smashing through a market full of rotten fish on a hot, humid summer afternoon. Something had *died,* I was sure of it.

I started mouth breathing in my panic to avoid the rankness, and then I became concerned about what was happening to my lungs and decided it was better not to breathe at all. Of all the hideous things that had offended my senses previously, and they were many and varied, I could not believe *how much worse* this was than any of them. It was the pits. And I was keeping a relatively safe distance from the source. The doctor was going to *die* when she got up close to it, and what a horrible way to go.

'Well, I was in bed with my boyfriend,' the patient explained, 'and he said it smelt bad and felt kind of weird, when we were . . .' she faltered, 'in bed.'

Oh my god. Her boyfriend . . . they were . . .

I didn't know why the patient wasn't passing out from sheer embarrassment, or proximity to the stink. Maybe it was like a fart. Maybe it didn't smell so bad to *her,* but I had never smelt anything so putrid in my entire life, and I had spent my last holiday in pungent Vietnam. The doctor constructed the necessary gynaecological scaffolding and shone a torch into the abyss as the woman asked curiously, 'Is there something in there? Is it a tampon?'

'Yep,' the doctor gasped, trying to limit speech and inhalation, as she extracted a sodden brown lump of cotton and string.

I opened the huge yellow medical waste bin, the doctor dropped it in and the lid slammed shut.

When the patient had dressed and gone to shower, and had been started on prophylactic antibiotics 'just in case', I found the Odour-Eater spray in the pan room, spritzed myself liberally with it, then bombed the patient's room until the floor was slick and the air was heavy with chemical vapour dew, and I could *still smell it*. It was like smoke from the nastiest fire ever burnt that went everywhere and permeated *everything*. The shower I had after work that day was like something you see in a movie where a radiation leak, or a rape, has occurred. So many layers of skin, so little time to remove them all.

'How was work?' I asked my boyfriend when he arrived home. He worked in an office; the grossest thing he happened upon in his place of work was usually along the lines of someone dropping a sly, noxious fart, or a long-abandoned lunch being discovered in the staffroom fridge. It was as the world *should* be.

'Eh.' He shrugged. 'It was okay, nothing special . . . And you?'

'If I tell you, you'll hate me,' I said.

'Then don't tell me! Please!' he replied urgently, and I laughed, but it got the better of him, as it always did. 'Okay, tell me,' he sighed. He knew he wasn't going to like it, but he couldn't help himself. And I guess if I had been a better person, I wouldn't have said anything, but that's just not my style.

'Well . . .' And I could see him turning a pale green as I told him the story in all its gloriously ugly, vivid detail. It was the tale of a smell so strong that it should have been a colour.

'Your job is *fucked*!' he said passionately, shaking his head in disgust.

'I know.'

'Seriously, I want to vomit right now!'

'I'm sorry,' I said, and I started to laugh.

Sharing the gruesome details made it better, almost made it worthwhile, in fact. If good old-fashioned repulsion was your thing, then I was the girl for you, even if every tampon advertisement made you flinch forever after and strong-smelling seafood brought a shudder forth from the depths of your soul.

Leo

You met all kinds of people in Detox. For every bum who lived on the street and could fit all of their worldly possessions into a plastic bag from Coles, there was a high-flying Icarus who was about to come crashing down to earth. For the bums, Detox was a step up in the world, with hot food, a warm bed and protection from the elements that plagued them, like winter and random, unprovoked assaults. For the others, it was a step down into the gutter, made under sufferance, and widely broadcast to all and sundry by the presence of a permanent sneer and complaints about the catering.

Leo was 62, but looked much older, and had the rich, plummy voice of a well-fed, well-educated homosexual. He was a retired professor of Fine Arts, or at least he claimed to be, and he said that the 'brutal ugliness' and 'void of talent' in contemporary art often brought him to tears, although it could have been all the vodka making him weepy, because people do tend to be more emotionally expansive with a litre and a half of Smirnoff on board.

'There's no poetry anymore, modern artists are *philistines*!' he said, bitterly.

He was sober once, for 15 years, which was nothing to sneeze at. He had started drinking again when his long-term partner died of an AIDS-related illness a decade earlier, and while he was a high-functioning alcoholic in his thirties, it was a different story in his fifties. The physical and mental decline was rapid and merciless. Leo said that he had retired from his job because he was so disheartened and 'aesthetically offended' by the new generation of artists and designers that he could not endure it any longer. But it was more than likely he was pushed or thrown out. Leo's brain was the equivalent of the sherry-soaked sponge layer in a trifle. He would have painted on the kitchen bench and eaten off a canvas if left to his own devices. He was damaged.

Over the last few years a lot of his friends had passed away, too, so he had not only lost his partner, but also his passion for his craft, his livelihood *and* his mates. He said that he was very lonely and alcohol helped him to forget. It helped him forget a little *too* well. Not just that he was lonely, but also his date of birth, and his address, and if he was allergic to anything. Filling out his admission paperwork was a ball-ache, and took five times longer than it needed to, but there was no real urgency because Leo wasn't going to be rushing off anytime soon. He had ataxia, the uneven ambulation that is eventually bestowed on all malnourished alcoholics, and had his work cut out just trying to walk in a straight line.

I first met Leo when he came into hospital with so much bruising to his face and body that he looked like a crushed grape, and I was surprised another patient didn't try to drink him.

'You'll have to use my other arm,' he said, as I was about to check his blood pressure. He pushed his sleeve up to show me all the old dark blood trapped under his pale, papery skin.

'What happened?' I asked, alarmed. 'You look like you were hit by a car!'

'Well, you probably won't believe this,' Leo said conspiratorially, 'but the other night I was walking through the city when a young man on a motorcycle suddenly mounted the footpath! I saw him run over a backpacker at the top of the street, she must have been *terribly* injured, and he didn't even stop! And he came flying down the street, right towards me, so I leapt out of the way and fell into a stairwell . . .' He trailed off. 'But the most peculiar thing is that the young man riding the motorcycle, he looked about 21, well, he was *completely naked*, except for a pair of translucent underpants. It was very strange.' Leo was genuinely baffled.

'Wow,' I said, stunned. 'That *is* unbelievable.'

This was my first encounter with the phenomenon of confabulation, the confusion of imagination and memory that occurred when your brain had been pickled in hard liquor for any significant length of time. The gaps in memory, caused by blackouts and brain damage, were distorted and puttied over with fantastic, often elaborately detailed, completely spontaneous bullshit. It was sadly sincere, unintentional fiction. Leo was telling the truth, it just wasn't the *truth*-truth.

On that first day Leo was a sweaty, tremulous, nervous wreck and, if you were a fan of repeating yourself a hundred times a day, then he was a dreamboat.

'I need to call my sister!' he said, panicked, as I was writing in his chart at the nurses' station.

'You called her half an hour ago,' I told him.

'Did I? Oh, goodness, I don't remember that . . . Are you sure?'

'Yeah, I dialled the number for you.'

'Oh.' He looked disappointed. 'Well, what did she say?'

'I have no idea, Leo, you're the one who spoke to her.'

He was crestfallen. 'Well, I haven't any money and I seem to have only the clothes I'm wearing . . . I think I need some Valium, I'm *terribly* anxious . . . I need to call my sister!'

I reminded Leo that I had given him medication an hour ago and we proceeded to have the same conversation we had *just had* for a second time, practically word for word. Leo called his sister ten times on his first day in hospital and I learnt that she was going to drop off some clothes, toiletries and money for him at least ten times as well.

'How are you today, Leo?' I asked each day, and his response never varied.

'Oh, I feel absolutely *dreadful*! I'm terribly, *terribly* anxious!' he complained, as his nervous system struggled to regain a sober equilibrium. He liked the Valium we were giving him to treat his withdrawal, though, and developed a Pavlov's dog-type response whenever he saw a nurse: he would wring his hands like a wet dishcloth and become visibly distressed. Even if some benzodiazepine love was forthcoming, he didn't remember five minutes later, so the angst train just rolled on and on. Leo was neurotic, but it was impossible to gauge how much of it could be apportioned to withdrawal, and how much was authentically him. I hoped that as his symptoms subsided, he would be slightly less precious and painful to be around. He wasn't.

Sometimes I felt guilty when I didn't warm to a particular patient, but some people were difficult to warm to. I didn't like everybody I worked with, either, and vice versa, and half the time I didn't even like my boyfriend, but you just had to try not to let it show. I felt sorry for Leo – he was a sad old man before his time, whose formerly full life had been gutted like a fish – but he got on my nerves. He was spectacularly self-absorbed, hijacking every compulsory recovery group and funnelling the broader, unrelated discussion back to *his* most pressing issues and persecutory personal demons. The absence of a short-term memory meant he failed to absorb any new information that came his way, so it didn't matter how many times he was informed that the groups were intended to be educational, rather than confessional, they all became 'The Leo Show' when his transient amnesia kicked in. It was the dullest show on earth. *He* found the subject matter compelling, obviously, but it bored the absolute tits off everybody else and he never noticed, of course.

After an enforced ten-day vacation in hospital, Leo was patched up and fattened up, his bruises ever so slowly fading. His body had taken such a beating in the last few years that its ability to heal was severely impaired and his dark purple bruises were lethargically becoming sickly shades of green and yellow. The doctors were concerned about him being at home alone – they felt he was an ongoing suicide risk as well as being physically unsound and more rickety than a broken chair – so they arranged for a social worker to call in and see him, which was basically code for surveillance and had more to do with avoiding charges of medical negligence than anything else. Leo said it was unnecessary, but that it would be nice to have a visitor. Even after ten days of food, rest and medication, he still looked haggard and unkempt. I shuddered to think what the interior of his house looked like, but I imagined it wasn't pretty, or particularly fragrant, and I felt very sorry for the social worker who was going to find out.

Leo surfaced at the hospital a few months later, re-toxed, in need of another detox and, again, covered in scratches, cuts and bruises. This time he was also sporting a huge black eye and a marked limp.

'*Oh my god*, Leo! You're a mess! What happened?' I asked him, horrified. He had lost a bunch of weight, was vaguely jaundiced and looked and smelled like he hadn't showered since I last saw him.

'Actually, I was extremely lucky to survive,' Leo explained, sombre as an undertaker. 'I was standing at the window in my front room watching the recent electrical storms, which were *quite* spectacular by the way, when a huge tree in the yard was struck by lightning and a branch suddenly came crashing through the window and hit me in the face! I was *showered* with glass, that's how I ended up with all these cuts, and luckily a neighbour heard me screaming for help . . . I was very fortunate. It's honestly a wonder that I wasn't electrocuted or crushed by the tree. I really should be *dead*!'

I read Leo's admission notes and the ambulance transcripts completed by the paramedics who had attended to him at the scene.

Found unconscious in front yard by neighbours, after falling through window. Numerous contusions, smells strongly of ETOH [ethanol], appears grossly intoxicated . . . Several empty vodka bottles found inside patient's home. Residence extremely unsanitary and filled with rubbish.

The doctors explained to Leo that his latest pathology results showed that his blood had turned to weak, watery soup, diluted by years of booze and carelessness, and warned him that one more decent fall or knock to the head would be the end of him if he continued to drink. He had come to the point of no return and now it was all down to him. He was aghast, and told every person with whom he crossed paths on the ward, including the tea lady and the cleaner, that he was mere inches from death.

'This was just the shock I needed to turn my life around,' he said, gravely. 'It's an extremely critical time.'

'Oprah would say it's an "a-ha!" moment!' one of the other patients suggested, when Leo cornered her in the hallway and detailed his precarious haematological state. He looked confused, and not for the first time that day.

'Who's Oprah?' he asked.

Leo had big plans for the future. He was adamant that he was going to give up drinking. He said he knew he could do it because he had been sober before, but he was going to talk to his GP about getting some Valium for his 'nerves', and he was going to see a counsellor, and go to Alcoholics Anonymous meetings, and then he was going to speak to his colleagues at the university about doing some work as a tutor on a part-time basis, to keep himself occupied . . .

Everybody except Leo could see that he was going to return home and drink himself to death, and that's exactly what he did. His funeral notice was in the newspaper a few months later. It was a sad, threadbare end to what must once have been a rich and colourful life. Oprah would have wept.

Albert

As far as I knew, Delirium Tremens was the name of an expensive Belgian beer sold at my local bottle shop, which contained 8.5% alcohol and got you drunk pretty fast.

I became aware of the *other* delirium tremens in my first few months working in Detox, and I liked the beer infinitely more than the medical condition, not least because of the inappropriateness of its name. Clinically speaking, delirium tremens, or 'the horrors', was a state of acute delirium that occurred as a result of severe alcohol withdrawal, and could be fatal. Naming a beer after it was like having a cigarette brand called Lung Adenocarcinoma. I would have found that amusing, too. In an ideal world, the delirium tremens patient would be medicated within an inch of their lives and spend a week comfortably sedated in a dimly lit, unstimulating environment, snoozing their craziness away, but that was never how it panned out in reality.

Albert was a sailor with decades-old tattoos bleeding out on his leathered arms, who had, for the last 40 years, happily split his days between drinking on his boat and drinking in his caravan. When his brother found him unconscious on the floor of the caravan, covered in ants and lying in a pool of rancid urine in 38°C heat, surrounded by a mountain of beer cans and garbage and a marvellous stench, time was finally called on his eternal summer.

As a detox candidate, Albert was an unknown quantity, since he hadn't gone a day in his adult life without a drink. This was his first attempt to stop, and it was a foregone conclusion that he and sobriety were not going to get along when they finally came face to face. He turned up to the hospital late on Sunday evening with his 'sea legs' on, he said, but really he was just so pissed he could hardly walk, and blew 0.43 on the breathalyser. He was pleasant and jovial at a staggeringly high reading, instead of dead like most people would be, but when the alcohol began to slowly leach from his body, Albert turned into somebody else. And *that* guy was the very definition of unreasonable.

It varied with each patient, but if things were going to turn pear-shaped and delirium tremens-y, you generally had an inkling by day two or three, and Albert began to lose his shit right on time. He thought it was 1986 and refused to stay in bed, even though his matchstick legs could barely hold him and his entire body shook like jelly on a plate. Instead, he careened wildly from side to side down the hallway in a stubborn attempt to get to the exit, and beyond. He grabbed at the handrail for support occasionally, or just crumpled weakly to the floor, where he would sit panting for a minute and point-blank refuse any offer of assistance.

'Albert, I have to do a lot of paperwork if you fall on the floor and start bleeding everywhere. Cut me some slack and let me help you, okay?' I said, and he looked right through me, eyes glazed and unfocussed and mumbling mutinously, physically present but otherwise absent.

By day four, Albert was officially in 'the DTs'.

Albert was adamant that he was feeling fine, but told me he was going to have to go home because the spiders and insects crawling all over the walls were really starting to bother him. I gave him some more medication.

People in the DTs often saw bugs and arachnids, and the visual hallucinations could be vivid and prolonged, and even more intense if they experienced formication, the feeling that something was crawling on or under their skin. They could spend hours scratching at nothing, shredding themselves to ribbons with their nails or whatever object was at hand. Albert scratched a little, but spent 90% of the day and night packing and unpacking his bag, and then repacking his bag, in preparation for his wishfully imminent departure from hospital. He had chartered a helicopter, he said. Then his mate from the army was going to bust him out, or else he was going to jump out the window and swim home. It wouldn't have been much of a swim if he had managed to pry open one of the deadbolted windows; we were on the fourth floor of an ugly brick building, only surrounded by a sea of concrete.

We fed Albert diazepam and quetiapine, an anti-psychotic medication, fistfuls of the stuff, but there was no respite. He didn't sleep or eat. He peed on the floor and shit the bed.

Occasionally it felt like he was making progress, drifting ever so slightly back to the surface, but people in the DTs were like bobbing apples in a tub, within your grasp one moment and submerged the next. Albert had brief periods of lucidity, telling me that he really needed to paint his boat and getting the year right when I asked, and then he was gone again, sitting on his bed, intently watching the blank wall in front of him like it was a widescreen television.

'Do you know where you are, Albert?' one of the other nurses asked him.

'What do you mean, *do I know where I am*? Get out of my fucken house!' he railed at her. 'Go on! *Get out*, ya dirty bastards!'

Albert walked unsteadily out to the nurses' station where I was standing behind the desk. He *seemed* calm, but he was unpredictable, so I moved a lamp and anything else with missile potential out of his reach and took a step back, hopefully beyond his swinging range.

'Hi, Albert,' I greeted him. 'What can I do for you?'

'G'day, love.' He smiled at me, as friendly as could be. 'I'll have a packet of Samboy Salt & Vinegar and a pot of VB thanks,' he said politely, reaching into the pocket of his grubby shorts and taking out a beaten leather wallet, which he began fumbling through, looking for money that wasn't there.

'Albert, you're in the hospital,' I told him. 'There's no beer here, and no chips.'

His face fell and he glared at me. 'You call this an RSL, with *no beer* and no fucken *chips*? Bloody hell!' He shook his head disgustedly, gave me one last withering look, then staggered back into his room.

He sat on the edge of his bed, fuming, incensed by the poor service and inferior facilities of our shit club, then reached for his bag and began packing. And unpacking.

Some of the nurses had a real knack with the difficult patients, which I was quietly in awe of. I had no patience and got fed up quickly. When Albert told *me* to fuck off, I would take him at his word and go and make myself a cup of coffee.

'Let me out of this fucken dump! I'm going home! My boat is parked outside and you do-gooder *cunts* can *FUCK OFF*! I'm leaving!'

Albert was half out of the door to his room. He was holding his freshly packed bag with one hand, except he had neglected to zip it up so his clothes were falling out on to the floor, and the other hand was clutching at the door jamb, keeping him vertical.

Tony, a tall nurse who had seen it all before, talked to Albert in the calm tone of a parent addressing a small child who was throwing an epic tantrum after a binge of refined sugar and artificial flavourings.

'Now, Albert, we've talked about this before. You're not well enough to go home yet,' Tony patiently explained.

'YES I FUCKEN AM! FUCK OFF!' Albert bellowed.

'Do you remember when I came into your room a few minutes ago? And you were trying to do a poo in the hand basin?'

Albert paused, and stood swaying on his feet as he absorbed this apparently surprising revelation.

'That's because you're not well, and that's why you need to stay in the hospital a bit longer.' Tony handed the glassy-eyed Albert a paper cup of sedatives and a glass of water. 'Now take these and go and have a little lie down,' he said gently.

Albert did as he was told, lying down on his bed and *finally* sleeping. He had been 'awake' for almost a week. Everybody was sick and tired of the constant observation, having to coax or bully him into swallowing medication and hovering by him in case he fell but not wanting to get too close, in case he suddenly threw a punch. It was exhausting.

'Peace at last!' I said, sitting down with a cup of tea to relish the first real lull since he had arrived on the ward. I even had time to make myself a piece of toast.

Of course, Albert only slept for 20 minutes and then he was off and racing.

His brother called every day to check on his condition.

'How is he?' he asked, sounding worried.

'He's a little bit better today,' I said, contorting rather than bending the truth: Albert was squatting in the corner of his room, swatting at imaginary flies and cursing non-existent enemies. Again.

For the first week, Albert was a maniac, and then there was a painfully slow plateau where he was more like a nursing-home patient, weak and dependent and unable to care for himself, but he gradually crawled out of the hole.

It took half an hour, and he had to use both hands, but he could finally get a cup to his mouth, and then he wanted to feed himself. The spoon hovered in the air in front of his face, time and time again, but his brain was too fried to perform the more delicate motor skill of steering cutlery into his open mouth. He quickly became exhausted, too tired to even hold his arm up, and I spoon-fed him mush like a toddler. Tears of frustration slid off his cheek and splashed on to my hand. It was no fun for anyone.

We gave Albert a shave and got him dressed. The physiotherapist brought a walker and Albert did his weird pony over-step around the ward, always veering wildly to the left, so much so that if left to his own devices he would just keep turning in a circle. His short-term memory was shit. He ate breakfast and then asked what time breakfast was, even though there was orange juice dribbling down his chin and porridge stuck to the front of his pyjamas.

He started to eat and drink independently, and with greater ease, and his concave face began to fill slightly. He knew the month and what year it was, but he didn't know who the prime minister was and didn't give a shit, either.

'Pack of fucken bastards, they're all the same.'

He may have been brain damaged, but he made a salient point.

In another week, Albert was the new and improved version of his previously skeletal self. He had been weaned off all the Valium and anti-psychotics and pumped full of vitamins, fluids, tea and biscuits. There was meat on his bones and even a slight rosiness to his cheeks. He was still fairly unsteady on his feet, but that was a legacy of his alcoholism and would not be as easily corrected.

His brother came to collect him and was stunned by the change. He hadn't seen Albert sober, or looking even vaguely healthy, in eons. It had been arranged for Albert to go into supported 'dry' accommodation in the country, where he would be kept away from alcohol and all meals would be provided. His caravan had been condemned by the council.

Fortunately or unfortunately, Albert recalled little of his demented three-week vacation, thanks to the truckload of drugs we had given him and a general decline in neurological function. Subsequently, *his* agenda post discharge from hospital was to go fishing and to the RSL for 'two or three pots'.

Albert had basically learnt nothing from his trip to hospital, but I had learnt that it was very difficult to teach an old drunk new tricks.

Callum

'Did you tick my name off? It's Callum. Make sure you tick me off! I don't want to get in trouble for not coming to lunch,' Callum said, overexcited as usual, like a giant puppy, when he sat down at the table across from me with a huge plate of food.

'Relax, Callum, I've ticked you off the list,' I replied.

'Good,' he said, and then started stuffing mounds of food into his gob, using his fork like a shovel.

I was supervising the patients as they ate lunch in the dining room, marking the attendance list and on watch in case anybody had a seizure, choked on their mashed potato, or decided it was a good idea to call the kitchen lady a moll. Usually, I just watched television and tuned out for half an hour while the patients hoovered up the hospital cuisine. Sometimes it was the first real meal they'd had in weeks, so they were generally preoccupied and well behaved and all about the eating.

But every so often, someone dropped to the floor and

flopped about like a goldfish that had jumped its tank, and I got to be a nurse instead of a babysitter. There was a cylinder of oxygen, a suction machine and a whole bunch of other medical equipment tucked away in the corner of the dining room for such occasions. Thankfully they didn't come around too often. Watching television was much more relaxing than rolling a convulsing patient onto their side and trying to prevent them biting off a chunk of their own tongue or aspirating on their own blood, saliva or vomit. When your body has adjusted over time to the constant presence of a substance like alcohol or benzodiazepines, and it is then suddenly absent, a worn nervous system can spontaneously lose its shit, and you run the risk of experiencing withdrawal seizures. You can have a tonic clonic, petit mal or grand mal seizure, or a combination of the different types, and they can last for a minute or so, and include fun things like tongue biting, frothing from the mouth, chipped teeth and incontinence. They can also last much longer than a minute, cutting off essential oxygen supply to the brain or blocking your airway, and the potential physical consequences become increasingly grave. And if you're really, *really* unlucky, you can die. People with a history of withdrawal seizures practically got a free pass into Detox in hospital because there was no way of telling if this was, or was not, the one time they might end up dead, which would be considered an 'unsatisfactory treatment outcome'. Of course it was still possible you might end up dead, even in hospital, but the odds were in your favour with all the doctors, nurses, drugs and medical equipment lying about the place.

When the kitchen ladies called out for seconds, Callum bounded out of his seat and returned with a reloaded plate and an extra bowl of dessert. It was going to take a while for him to get through it, because he wouldn't shut up. All the other patients had finished up, scraped their plates clean and headed downstairs, and it was only Callum left, eating and talking, chatting and shovelling, and I couldn't leave until he was done.

Callum had blond hair, blue eyes and was almost six feet tall, a gangly 18-year-old who looked sweet and innocent, but this choirboy had some serious track marks on his arms and burns on his neck where somebody had held lit cigarettes to him. He had been robbing houses since he was 12 and started using heroin when he was 15. His dad was his dealer and was one of the first people arrested for importing heroin from Asia in the seventies, Callum told me, a little proud of his family's infamy. I guess it is nice to know that your dad was a trailblazer, even if it was for something like heroin trafficking and he wasn't good enough at it to avoid getting caught.

Callum had just been released from a juvenile detention centre where he'd spent some time courtesy of holding up a corner store. He was charged with stealing, instead of armed robbery, because he had asked the cashier, 'Could you please give me the money?' and hadn't demanded it.

He gave the cashier a choice, his barrister said, and she *chose* to give him the contents of the till. It had all been caught on CCTV, including the bit where Callum had apologised while he was holding her up, saying, 'Sorry to do this to ya, love, but it's just bad luck that you were working today. You're not too traumatised, are ya?'

'No, I actually feel quite relaxed,' the girl had replied.

'That's good, love.'

Callum said that there were ways of doing things and just because you're a thieving bastard and a junkie doesn't mean you have to be a rude prick, too.

'I guess that's where having good manners really pays off,' I said.

'Dead set.' He nodded. Next time, though, he was going to grown-up jail, guaranteed.

Antiques were Callum's favourite things to steal.

'I'm really into antiques. I love 'em,' he told me. I asked him how he knew where to find antiques worth taking, how he knew which houses to hit.

'I've got connections,' he said mysteriously.

'What kind of connections?'

It turned out he had a pretty sweet arrangement. His friends were real estate agents and insurance salesmen. They gave him the address and descriptions of the valuable stuff, he did the breaking and entering, and they split the takings 70/30. Callum was taking the bigger risk so he got the bigger cut.

He gave me the benefit of his knowledge and expertise in burglary and advised me how to best safeguard my home from people like him.

'That Crimsafe mesh is shit. Proper metal bars on the windows, that's what you need. And forget about any kind of rolling door locks. Unless you've got a dead lock with a key, any other lock is a fucken waste of time. It takes me four seconds to get in, *max*.'

He was very enthusiastic about his craft. 'Oh, yeah, and if you're gonna do a ram raid, you've gotta head out of the city,' he continued knowledgeably, before instructing me on how to break bulletproof glass and outsmart sensor alarm systems.

'I love crime,' he said, happily. 'I don't even do it for the money anymore. But I'm getting too cocky.'

He said that he felt bad stealing stuff sometimes, like when he and his mate had broken into a house to get an antique sword that had just been valued and insured. Callum could tell they were poor.

'Everything in their place was shit. Like they had this tiny television and all the furniture was old, but not like antique old, just *crap*.' He had an argument with his mate, who wanted to take the sword anyway, and Callum told him he could do what he wanted but he wasn't taking it and climbed back out the window. His mate had followed him, reluctantly, and as they were walking back home at two in the morning, a police car had pulled up beside them.

'What are you doing out here?' the cops had asked.

'We're looking for a lost dog,' Callum said automatically.

The cops split them up, and Callum told them he was looking for a labrador named Lucky and his mate said he was looking for a blue heeler called Chad.

'You're looking for different dogs, you haven't even got your stories straight!' the cops said when they brought them back together.

'We're looking for *two* dogs,' Callum said, without hesitation. Lying was a reflex.

The cops searched them, found nothing, and had to let them go.

'We know you're lying, you little smart-arses. If we see you out here again, we're taking you to the watch house,' the cops warned them, and then drove off.

'See?' Callum said to me. 'If we'd robbed the sword, we would have got done for it. That's fucken karma,' he continued. 'You don't steal shit from poor people.'

I looked over at the clock. 'Dude, pick up the pace! We haven't got all day. Hurry up and finish your food,' I said.

'Oh, yeah.' He grinned at me, then reached for his first bowl of banana cake and custard and told me another dog story. He was a good storyteller and I was a good audience for him. It was a much more entertaining lunch supervision than most.

He had wanted half an ounce of weed and his dealer wanted a pedigree boxer puppy for her daughter's birthday so Callum had arranged a swap, and told her he would get her a dog in exchange for the weed. He looked online, found a breeder and called him to ask if he could take a look at the new litter. The guy gave him his address, and Callum asked how much he was selling them for.

'Five hundred each,' the breeder told him.

'I've only got a hundred . . .' Callum replied and the guy laughed at him.

'Tough luck, then,' he said, and promptly hung up.

Callum called a taxi and when they pulled up to the

breeder's house, Callum told the driver that he was going in to get his grandmother's puppy back, because someone had stolen it.

The taxi driver wasn't keen on having a dog in the car. 'We only allow service dogs,' he had said uneasily, and Callum started crying.

'But they're going to sell it!' he protested. 'Please, you've got to help me! I told my grandmother I'd get her dog back! *Please!*'

The driver relented, taken in by Callum's crocodile tears and seamless bullshit. 'Oh, okay then . . .'

And Callum ran into the backyard, grabbed a brindle puppy and jumped into the back seat with it.

'Go, go, *go*!' he said, and the taxi driver went.

'That's a very nice dog,' the driver commented, as Callum nursed the puppy on the drive home.

'Yeah, he's worth a lot of money, that's why they took him. My grandmother's gonna be really happy.'

He got dropped off a block from his dealer's house and carried the tiny puppy to its new home. She gave him his half-ounce and he gave her the dog. Three days later it died of parvovirus. The dealer called Callum and demanded he get her another puppy.

'No way! I already got one. It's not my fault your dog died,' he told her.

He shook his head in disbelief. 'She paid $300 for the immunisations and everything. *Unreal.*'

When Callum left the hospital a few days later, he gave me a hug goodbye.

'I reckon you'll remember me when I'm gone,' he said.

'Yeah, I think you're right,' I told him. 'It's been educational.'

He was going to start an apprenticeship as an electrician if his interview the next day went well. He was a smart kid, now seven days clean, but he was going home to his dad's place, and his dad's heroin, so his future wasn't as bright as it should have been.

The next time he came into Detox, about six months down the track, he didn't have the same enthusiasm for getting clean, or telling stories, and only stayed for a day and a half.

Chris P Bacon

I don't know what name he was given as a baby, but he didn't think it suited him as an adult so he changed it a couple of times until it 'felt right'. It was fairly straightforward. All you had to do was fill out a few forms, pay $160 and you could reboot your entire existence, even if your choice of name inadvertently revealed a history of mental illness that possibly should have restricted your access to deed poll in the first place. Presenting, Mr Chris P Bacon.

Chris P was a sweet guy with the unenviable burden of schizophrenia. I met him when I volunteered to spend a half-day a fortnight giving depot medications, slow release anti-psychotics administered via injection, to a roster of mental health patients, just to get out of Detox for a little while. Chris P was the only one who turned up religiously, and I liked him a lot. I prepared the drug, he took his injection like a man, and then we watched TV for a couple of hours. I checked his blood pressure and pulse every 30 minutes and kept an eye out for an adverse reaction.

Apparently some patients in Mexico or Japan had slumped into spontaneous comas after the same type of injection, but Chris P was well into his second year of being jabbed and, so far, still conscious. I was glad. An unexpected coma sounded like a drag, and we had much to learn from Dr Phil.

Chris P had smoked a boatload of dope since his early teens, until he went 'a bit crazy' and, depending on who you asked, the drugs either gave him schizophrenia, or provided a portal for dormant schizophrenia to emerge. As far as was known, there was no history of it, or any other serious mental illness, in his family. Chris P had been on a multitude of medications over the years, and in and out of hospital for the last decade while dosages were titrated between sub-therapeutic and fatal. He had eventually stabilised, and the 18-month period of regular injections was the longest he had gone without a hospital admission. Even so, he still seemed very far away sometimes. He became distant and distracted mid conversation, preoccupied by internal stimuli, because his auditory hallucinations never stopped.

Sometimes it was a single voice, he said, like someone was talking to him, or abusing him, if the voice was derogatory and cruel. Other times it was non-stop chatter in his head, like he was listening to the constant murmuring of a television set in the background, and sometimes it was loud clamour, like a stockmarket floor. All of the choices available to him sounded shitty to me.

The litre and a half of wine he drank every other day wasn't doing a lot for his general health, neither was a diet primarily consisting of frozen meat pies and sausage rolls, but alcohol quietened the voices, even if it didn't shut them up altogether.

'Sometimes I just want some peace and quiet,' he said.

I couldn't imagine what it would be like to never, ever have a moment to yourself; the thought of it made my skin crawl. All I could think of was that it would be like having a visitor come to stay, who you didn't even like, and who *never fucking left*. On the whole, I was a solitary animal. I liked people, but I *really* liked not being around them all the time. And if alcohol was my only hope of solitude, the one thing that made everything fall away like slow-cooked meat from a bone, I would have been driven to drink, too. Plus, drunkenness was infinitely preferable to suicide, which he had attempted a couple of times. He figured that death was silent. For his sake, I hoped so.

I'd had the same boyfriend, minus a couple of breaks, since the third and final year of my nursing degree. My university attendance was so patchy and my attitude to study so half-arsed, neither one of us could believe that I was ever deemed competent to be let loose on the world, especially when I kept getting the names for arm and leg bones mixed up and was still pretty hazy on what kidneys were for. I told my friends and family to stay well.

My boyfriend was there when I got my first hospital pay, which seemed like a fortune, and accompanied me to the supermarket where I blew 200 bucks on cheese, crackers and alcohol after three years of scrimping and being poor.

My impulsive extravagance was somewhat novel then, as was my disregard for things that didn't interest me, like bank statements, or living within my means. I suspect that my boyfriend thought he could teach me the error of my ways, but unfortunately for him that didn't really interest me either.

He stuck around until five years later, when I was the same unreasonable, unrealistic person I had always been, but it was no longer endearing or entertaining. After a year of living together, cracks like chasms appeared between us, and all the love fell out. Familiarity had successfully bred contempt, like a million bitter, pissed-off bunny rabbits running riot over our relationship, and when we finally had the *big* fight, after tiring re-runs of the same fights we always had, it only took an evening for him to move out. All that remained were the bare spaces in the dust where his stuff had been. Neither one of us had been particularly houseproud.

As soon as the deed was done, the release of tension and pressure gave way to a flood of pain and all of the reasons I had for breaking up with him conveniently deserted me in my hour of need. I wasn't happy *with* him, but now I was fucking *miserable* without him. I sucked on a bottle of gin, smoked half a pack of cigarettes and wailed down the phone to my best friends. Nothing much helped, because breaking up is a special kind of kick in the guts, the crappy gift that keeps on giving, and no amount of alcohol can dilute it, although I always try. My hurt and addled brain then kicked into survival mode and came up with the horseshit idea that reconciliation was the only scratch for my itch, despite the fact that I had cumulatively scratched all my skin off over the last year as our relationship disintegrated. What I really wanted was for the pain to stop, and for it to stop *immediately*, even though the only effective medicine for my woe was the imperceptibly slow passing of time, and a hot friend of a friend on Facebook. Five years was a long time to be with someone, but I have never been one of those moderate people who can maintain a friendship in the aftermath. It was all or nothing, and I could live with nothing. Which was fantastic, because it's what I had.

I tried to focus on the positives and, on the plus side, my wardrobe space had instantly doubled and I could sleep spreadeagled in the middle of the bed if I wanted to, which I did. On the negative, I was a bawling, ugly, red-eyed mess. *Wanting* to break up with someone and *actually breaking up* are two very different animals. One feels like a really good idea and the other does not feel good at all.

I cried my eyes out and stayed awake most of the night, but I still had to go to work the next day because schizophrenia doesn't care about my feelings, and Chris P was expecting me.

I turned up to the hospital the next morning hungover, hysterical on the inside and looking like a bag of shit, to put it mildly. My eyes were bloodshot and puffy and my face was pale as chalk. I didn't have the energy or inclination to even pretend I was okay. I just put one foot in front of the other and tried not to cry.

'What's wrong?' Chris P asked me.

'I broke up with my boyfriend last night,' I told him.

'Oh, don't worry!' he said brightly, smiling at me encouragingly. 'There's plenty more fish in the sea!'

In a kind attempt to comfort me, Chris P told me that he'd had a girlfriend once, a couple of years ago, but things hadn't really worked out with her, either. She had multiple personalities – one of them was a little French girl with an accent and everything – and *all* of her personalities had refused to take medication. They had an argument at his flat one afternoon and she had called the police, claiming that he had threatened to kill himself. With a history like his, he didn't think there was much point protesting, so he went peacefully to the hospital for a mandatory assessment. He had given her his bankcard as he left, and asked if she could at least pay the rent for him, and she said she would, but she didn't. And she didn't *just* not pay the rent, she also drained his bank account, stole everything of value from his flat and hocked all of his stuff at Cash Converters. The only thing left when he got home the next morning was his bed, and even that was minus the sheets and pillows.

'Wow, that is *cold*,' I said to him. 'I'm sorry. That's really horrible.'

'Yeah, it wasn't a very good relationship,' he said, after some consideration.

Back in the days when he was very unwell and see-sawing, the faces on money would come alive and tell him to jump in front of a train or a bus, and Chris P believed that he could read people's minds, but if people asked him if he was hearing voices, he would shake his head vigorously.

'Oh, no, not at all,' he would say. Then elaborate, 'The Holy Spirit talks to me, but *that's it*! I only hear the voice of God.'

Chris P didn't ask for much from life and he barely got that. He had a wish list, and on it was a new bicycle and free trips to the dentist, but what he really wanted was a girlfriend, one who wasn't sick or crazy.

'That would be nice,' he said, but he didn't meet many girls. His Bible study group meetings were mostly male. He was pretty into the Bible and carried a pocket-sized one in his backpack, plus a bunch of Jehovah's Witnesses pamphlets in case somebody wanted one. Lately he had been tagging along on some of the suburban doorknocking missions, but only in an observational capacity.

'Maybe I'll meet a girl that way,' he said.

'What, when you're out doorknocking?'

'Yeah,' he said. 'There are a lot of women at home during the day. They might like to have a cup of coffee.'

I hesitated. 'Yeah, maybe.' It wasn't exactly kosher, but the thought of him checking out housewives as he spread the good word made me smile.

He became really sick when he was 19, so Chris P never really had the opportunity to hold down a regular job. He had a full-time job just keeping his shit together and his bones out of hospital. He had volunteered in a soup kitchen for a while and for Meals on Wheels, but eventually they had asked for a criminal check, and he had a decent record. When he had been psychotic and unmedicated, he had been hauled into the watch house for a number of transgressions, most of them revolving around being really intoxicated and the girl he was obsessed with at the time.

She lived across the street and he felt they had a very strong psychic connection because she sent him messages through the television and whatever music he was listening to. She was in love with him, and he knew he could love her too, but they were going to have to step it up and start communicating face to face instead of through household appliances, because he couldn't hug a kettle or a toaster. So he had waited all day outside her house, writing long letters about his feelings and his thoughts on marriage, and how many children they should have. It was dark when she finally came home from work and he didn't understand why she screamed so loud when he tried to give her a hug. It wasn't even a *loving* scream.

Chris P told me that he had heard about a cool job working with animals. His cousin had two fluffy white dogs and there was a dog beauty salon where she took them to get shampooed, blow-dried and even have their nails painted. He thought that would be quite a good way to make a living.

'That does sound pretty awesome,' I agreed, as I stuck a giant needle in his backside, delivering the magic drugs that kept him grounded and stopped him flying off into inner space, like a kid letting go of a balloon.

Pass the Parcel

Professionally speaking, I have a 12-month attention span. I get restless after a year. I liked working in Detox, so it took longer than it usually would for me to become bored, but it was inevitable. I took a related position in the Emergency Department, conducting drug and alcohol 'brief interventions', incidental counselling and education for people who had ended up in hospital for any number of reasons.

My job was to give people advice and treatment information if they wanted it, to point out the possible link between the bottle of overproof rum they had consumed and the eye gouging or fall from a table that followed, and to cop it on the chin when they told me to fuck off. I imagine the sense of accomplishment and job satisfaction was on par with doorknocking Mormons, in that there were few instances where you felt your message was being received, rather than endured. The aim of the game, though, was to 'plant the seed' of behavioural change while you had a captive, mostly steaming drunk, audience, prostrate and imprisoned in a supportive neck brace. Planting a seed is probably the most underwhelming stage of the agricultural growth cycle, and this was, too. There was very little visible yield for your efforts, but at least being based in the Emergency Department was interesting. Some days it was like being at the circus, a really gross, shitty circus perhaps, but a circus nonetheless.

I felt like a travelling salesman a lot of the time, fronting up uninvited to the bedside of patients who *looked* like they might have a substance abuse problem, or presented with conditions that *could* be drug and alcohol related, like assaults or a fall. It was basically a crappy lucky dip, and sometimes you hit substance-using paydirt without even trying, and other days you just hit a wall. Every jackass with a substance in their system was my bread and butter, but if it was quiet, I talked to anybody and everybody. I could tell within five seconds of introducing myself as a drug and alcohol nurse if I was wildly off the mark, because the non-users just stared at me, either wide-eyed and bewildered or a little paranoid and afraid, like maybe I knew something they didn't. You could smell the booze on the drinkers, and the opiate abusers were pretty conspicuous: they were either on a trolley having an overdose reversed, sat slumped in a chair on the nod, under arrest and police chaperone, or were attempting to abscond with a cannula in situ for a few days of injecting ease. A patent cannula was hot shit, a wedged-open doorway to a disintegrating network of veins which, after being repeatedly pricked and flooded with all sorts of nasty chemicals, eventually collapsed like sandcastles.

I had my own phone, so the other nurses or doctors in Emergency could reach me when one of my 'friends' turned up.

'I've got a customer for you,' the nurse at triage would say.

'Is it the guy shouting in the waiting room who smells like piss and can hardly stand up?'

'Yep, that's the one.'

'Okay, thanks.'

It was like a game of pass the parcel, and I understood why the triage nurses were pleased to see me. It was nothing personal. They were happy because when I turned up they could pass the parcel, which often times was a pretty ripe-smelling derelict with a massive deficit in social skills and attitude to burn. Their problem instantly became my problem, and they figured that since nobody had put a gun to my head to make me work with drunks and junkies in the first place, I deserved everything I got, as though I had more of an appetite for belligerent, incontinent, intoxicated people than most. I was fairly sure I didn't.

If, at any time during the conversation that followed, my new friend said the magic words, 'I am going to kill myself,' then I got to pass the parcel too, directly to Mental Health for psychiatric clearance. Or they could say the *other* magic words, 'I am going to kill *you*,' and they would be gifted to security, who re-gifted them to the police, who then ended up with the worst, most pissed-off present ever.

'I don't know how you can do your job,' other nurses would say to me, shaking their heads in disbelief, as I prepped the breathalyser to find out exactly *how* drunk a drunk I was dealing with. I shrugged. I wasn't great with body fluids, or stomas, or sick children, or acute mental illness. Blood didn't really bother me, but things being on the outside of bodies instead of in their proper place on the inside, bothered me a lot. Anything that prolapsed, open wounds where layers of white fat or muscle were visible, or watching nylon thread being pulled taut during suturing, made me feel lightheaded, and I had to go and sit down somewhere before I fell down in a faint. In drug and alcohol I got more verbal abuse, for sure, but substantially less gore and *actual* shit to deal with, and I liked it that way.

'I've done worse,' I said, and it was true. My mantra, when I felt my perspective slipping, was 'graft versus host, graft versus host', and I was just grateful not to be dealing with that type of thing anymore, no matter how much grief I got when I couldn't instantly fix a lifetime of general chaos, poor decision-making or self-inflicted brain damage.

Luckily, there are a lot of specialty areas in nursing, and you can just keep going until you find one that doesn't *completely* turn your stomach, or you can cut your losses and start looking for an entirely different career. Opening a café seemed to be a popular out.

One night in my first year in the Bone Marrow Unit, one of the nurses, who had been working there for about 25 years, asked me to give her a hand with one of her patients. He had a scorching high temperature, but was too incapacitated to swallow a tablet or any dissolvable paracetamol. That left intravenous paracetamol, which was crazy-expensive and in sparse supply in the hospital, and rectal paracetamol. Maureen had the Panadol suppository in her gloved hand and was liberally applying KY jelly to the tip when I walked into the room, gloved, gowned and ready to roll the guy over like a log.

'You know, sometimes I think I could have been a florist. I think I really would have enjoyed it . . . I've always loved gardening, I could have had a little shop,' she said to me, in a tone stranded somewhere between whimsy and bitterness. It was three thirty in the morning and I obviously wasn't the only person who pondered their career options in the dark hours.

'Yeah, that would have been nice,' I said, as I rolled the comatose patient onto his side and held him there.

'Or a coffee shop, that would have been good, too. Or a tea place, with scones and sandwiches . . .' she said, as she re-positioned the patient's leg.

'Like Devonshire teas, you mean?' I asked her.

'Yeah, that sort of thing. Morning tea and afternoon tea, with tablecloths and proper teapots, and little silver tongs for the sugar cubes,' she said, as she held the patient's bum cheeks apart and slid the suppository in. It got sucked in by gravity, or whatever, and disappeared, taking Maureen's sweet alternative reality with it.

It was wall-to-wall dickheads in Emergency sometimes. Actually, it was wall-to-wall dickheads a *lot* of the time. I was appalled and intrigued in equal amounts at the start, but after a month or two of such close proximity to trauma and chaos, and the same people turning up in the same trashed condition, it began to feel like *Groundhog Day*. I had seen this particular alcoholic patient for a number of variations on the same theme: broken nose, facial fracture, fall from standing height, gastritis from drinking methylated spirits, suspected pancreatitis . . . To give him his due, at least he mixed it up a bit. That made it ever so slightly more interesting for me, which was good of him.

'I know you, don' I?' the leering drunk (noun *and* verb) said, rolling around on the trolley, stinking of urine and with the front of his filthy trousers already covered in a dark, spreading stain.

'Yep.'

'Aye, I *knooow youuuu*! Whazyername, luv?'

'Kristy,' I told him. The same as it was last week, and the week before that.

'Lissen, Christine, I need tae make a phone call,' he said, and little bits of spit flicked out of his mouth and landed on me. I took a step back, trying to be subtle about it, and wondered how many different kinds of germs were currently sitting on my face.

'I need tae call me mam and letter know I'm siiick,' he drawled, then suddenly stopped talking and got this dreamy, faraway look in his eyes. He let out a long fart, which was immediately followed by a terrible smell and the spatter of soupy diarrhoea hitting the floor. I legged it out of there, gagging, and hurried off to the bathroom to disinfect my hands and face and any other part of me that may have made contact with any part of him. I looked in the mirror, at the foolishly non-waterproof mascara running down my face, with my skin turning bright pink from vigorous scrubbing, and thought, *Surely, there's a more pleasant way to make a living than this. There has to be.*

Sometimes I fantasised about working at Starbucks, where the only brown liquid I was likely to be exposed to was spilt macchiato, or caramel drizzle. Coffee smells nice, tastes delicious and makes you feel good. Coffee is never going to ask you to call its mother in Aberdeen, Scotland, and then shart in your presence.

Emergency wasn't always doom and gloom and diarrhoea, though. Sometimes it was the greatest show on earth and I was happy just to have a front-row ticket. Other people's embarrassment was my not-so-secret guilty pleasure, and I could usually find something or someone to laugh at if I wandered around the department long enough. I tried to be discreet, which, in an ideal world, would mean walking around the corner and out into the corridor before I collapsed into fits of laughter, but it didn't always happen.

One morning, a twenty-something patient asked if he could use a phone to call his boss. He needed to let him know that he wouldn't be coming in to work that day because he'd had 'a bit of an accident'.

He tried to speak quietly, but apparently his boss was on a mobile phone and was having difficulty hearing him, so the patient was forced to repeat himself, and loudly.

'Ah, yeah, mate, I'm in the hospital. I, uh . . . I broke my dick.'

The laughter from the other end of the phone could be heard from a distance of several metres.

'No, mate, I'm *serious*! I really did! I broke my dick!'

There was more laughter from the guy's boss, and everybody else who was within earshot of the conversation. Until that moment, I hadn't known it was even *possible* to fracture a penis, and I was struck by the shortcomings of my nursing degree and its bullshit curriculum. How many other hilarious medical conditions was I yet to be made aware of? Clearly, my university had failed me, just as I had failed it, with my complete lack of professionalism and by dissolving into uncontrollable giggling at the thought of a broken cock. And the laughs didn't stop there. An occurrence like a fractured penis lowered the tone of the department for the rest of the day and got the nurses rolling out all their favourite gross-out Emergency anecdotes, like the 17-year-old who had presented with abdominal pain. When asked if she was sexually active, she had replied, 'Nah, I just lie there,' which was amusing enough. But then her X-ray had come back, and apparently there was a scrunched up Samboy Salt & Vinegar chip packet wedged up in her vagina. Her boyfriend had run out of condoms, so they had sensibly eaten the chips first, then used the empty packet as a sheath, and she *had* actually been wondering what happened to it, so the mystery was now solved. And then there was The Saucepan, which was my favourite hospital story so far.

A couple presented to the triage desk in the middle of the night and the woman had a bloody tea towel pressed to her forehead, while the man accompanying her looked sheepish and slightly terrified.

'What have you got under there?' the nurse asked the woman, who gingerly removed the tea towel to reveal a large gash on her forehead, which was still trickling blood and had already swollen up like an apple.

'Ouch! How did you do that?' the nurse enquired.

'Um,' the woman said.

'Um,' the man said. Neither of them was keen to elaborate, which seemed suspicious.

'What happened?' the nurse asked again, and the woman looked at the man, and the man turned red and said, 'It's hard to explain,' followed by an awkward silence.

'It's really embarrassing . . .' he stalled, and the woman got sick of waiting for him to grow some balls.

'I'm epileptic,' she said, so the nurse figured she had a seizure, fell and hit her head but the woman told the truth, the whole truth and nothing but the truth.

'Okay . . .'

'And . . . well, we were having sex in the kitchen and I guess I had a seizure because I bit down on his . . . *thing* . . . so he hit me in the head with a saucepan.'

'She was clamped on like a rabbit trap!' he said defensively. 'I couldn't get her off!'

You couldn't *dream* this stuff up. Some days I laughed so hard I got a stitch.

Louis & Jeanette

My transient role in Emergency was a refreshing change of pace, but after a while I noticed that the drop in, drop out nature of my job severely eroded any chance of forming a meaningful rapport with the patients I saw. It was a foreign experience for me. Stays in Bone Marrow Transplant that lasted from months to years became stays of days to weeks in Detox, and finally minutes to hours in Emergency. Repetition was often the only means of creating any kind of bond, and seeing the same names and faces day after day made you feel impotent rather than helpful.

One of the most frustrating things about nursing is that the people you see repeatedly are usually stubbornly unwell and more than likely to die before their time. You practically develop amnesia when it comes to the patients who went home healed, if not cured, because the ones who didn't are burned into your brain, taking up most of the space. Sometimes when a patient was discharged from Oncology or Detox, I would wave goodbye to them saying, 'I hope I never see you again!' But I meant it in the nicest possible way.

Louis and Jeanette were chalk and cheese Emergency regulars who I saw more frequently than my parents, but had very little to do with in a clinical sense. They were both mental health patients, primarily, but that was it as far as common ground went. Louis was sweet, although he could be mean, and Jeanette was mean but could *probably* be sweet, although I never saw it for myself at the hospital.

Louis's true calling in life may well have been as a piece of Emergency waiting room furniture because he was there *all the time*, or at least it felt that way. Whenever his name appeared on the computer screen or I saw him approaching the counter, I heard The Replacements song 'Here Comes A Regular' in my head and wondered what he was going to say. Most of his presentations to Emergency began in the same fashion. The triage nurse would greet him by name, 'Hi, Louis. What can I do for you?'

And Louis would blurt out, 'I need to see a doctor!' as though a life, presumably his, hung in the balance.

'Why? What's the problem?' the nurse would ask.

'I'm not schizophrenic! I've been given the wrong diagnosis! You need to stop my medication!' was one reply, as was, 'My penis has shrunken!' And, memorably, 'There's something hard in my nose!' which was true, but it was only snot. Louis's default setting was catastrophic thinking, so the smallest ailment always blew up into a Cuban missile- or Tampa refugee-scale crisis. A mosquito bite meant malaria, and a grazed knee imminent gangrene, while a shrunken penis was 'a message from God that masturbation is a sin', and apparently had nothing to do with any of the notoriously dick-shrinking psychiatric medications he was on, or winter's cooler weather. Louis never presented complaining that he was lonely, or bored, but I think that was most often the case. It seemed like he just wanted some company, to be around other people for a while. He lived alone in a unit a few blocks from the hospital, but he spent most of his time pinballing from the Emergency Department to the Mental Health ward, and when he had temporarily worn out his welcome in one or both, from hospital to hospital, ad nauseam. He practically worked full-time at getting himself admitted to any place that would have him, ensuring his needs for food, beverages and socialisation were taken care of.

Louis *was* schizophrenic, and would admit to it most of the time. He had been on medication for decades and was fairly stable, although stable was a relative term. Louis may have been pretty nuts compared to most people, but not when he was compared with previous incarnations of himself. All in all, Louis was doing well because he was still alive and kicking. He had his own fatigued case manager, regular shock therapy for his depression and the energy to front up to Emergency most days. He knew that he had a captive audience at the hospital and that the nurses were going to listen to him, whether they liked it or not.

★

Whenever I turned up to work in the morning, there was patient 'potluck' in the Emergency waiting room: pissed people were passed out in chairs with their necks bent at seriously uncomfortable angles, old people were parked in wheelchairs waiting for their names to be called out, and there was always some early morning cyclist in lycra who was missing a couple of layers of skin after kissing asphalt with their body or face. 'Emergency' was a term that was very loosely interpreted by the general public. To me, an emergency was something potentially life-threatening and along the lines of electric shock, being hit by a car, having something explode on or near you, being stabbed or shot, pissing blood unexpectedly, having a heart attack or stroke or any of the million and one variations that might result in a person winding up dead without medical intervention. Many folks, however, disagreed, and rather than going to see their regular doctor, presented to the hospital with their pissant symptoms, and *then* expected people not to laugh at them, which I thought was a little rich. One guy came in complaining of 'a runny nose'. As in, 'Can you please pass me a tissue? I have a runny nose.'

I shit you not.

Most mornings, I bought a coffee at the hospital café before I started work. I had a bad habit of going to bed late, then sleeping in, and turning up to my place of work in a condition that was several fathoms from awake. Even though I had a perfectly good coffee machine at home, I rarely got my arse out of bed in time to use it. My brain seemed to believe that I lived in Europe. It was wide awake at night and a burnout in the morning, which wasn't terribly helpful.

The café at the hospital made the worst 'coffee' I had ever tasted. It was generally bitter, burnt and tepid, or else it was scorching hot with a skin on top because the milk had been boiled to the temperature of lava. Beggars could not be choosers, though, and the café had a captive market. There was nowhere else to buy coffee, and their desperate customers were primarily shift workers; people, like me, who were constantly knackered and fuelled by caffeine. The hospital was a sick utopia for profiteers. The many-storey car park that charged every visitor a king's ransom if they dared visit their loved ones was owned by a bunch of doctors, who showed no mercy and made no exceptions. 'Oh, your wife's in a coma in Intensive Care, and has been for a month? *Tough shit!* It's 50 dollars a day.'

One morning as I was yawning and waiting for my unimpressive yet essential coffee, I heard loud crying coming from the Emergency waiting room. It sounded like a man, too, which was even more unnerving. I guessed there had been a trauma overnight, a horrible car accident with multiple fatalities, or a fire, and I felt a little sick. Public outpourings of raw grief always made my stomach flip.

I walked hesitantly into the waiting room holding my sub-par flat white, expecting to see a bereaved family comforting each other, and all I saw was Louis, sitting in a chair right at the back, howling. I was relieved, but also confused, because Louis wasn't so much crying as *mimicking* crying. There were no tears in his eyes, or streaming down his cheeks, but his face was all scrunched up as he emitted his deafening bawl. As usual, I felt an inappropriate urge to laugh. There were a few other patients in the waiting room who were either fidgeting uncomfortably or pretending to be hearing impaired and ignoring Louis. All of them studiously avoided making any eye contact with him. When the triage nurse called out his name, Louis shut up for a second, then resumed his noisy lamentation as he shuffled over to the window and hovered there miserably.

'What's wrong, Louis?' the nurse asked him.

He couldn't, or wouldn't, talk.

'Do you have pain?' she enquired, and still, no response.

'Do you want me to call Mental Health?' she prompted, and Louis nodded yes, and let out a fresh howl.

'Okay, Louis, walk it off. Do a couple of laps of the waiting room and try to relax,' she said, kindly. 'I'll let the psych team know you're here.'

Poor Louis began slowly padding around the perimeter of the waiting room, 'crying' the whole time, and the room suddenly cleared, just like it did when somebody vomited or crapped their pants or started bleeding all over the place. There was something very confronting about a grown man bawling like a baby in public, and it didn't seem to agree with many people.

'What's up with Louis?' I asked the nurse, as one of the doctors came to investigate the racket, spotted Louis out in the waiting room and groaned loudly.

'He missed his shock therapy. He's been doing this all week.'

'Oh, *no* . . .'

A man approached the triage window and said awkwardly, 'Um, I think I'll try to get an appointment with my GP instead . . .'

'So will I,' the woman standing behind him piped up. They both seemed very ill-at-ease.

'Oh, are you sure?' the nurse asked, concerned. 'It really shouldn't be too much longer before you see a doctor.'

'Uh, yeah, we're sure,' they said, and promptly left.

Louis was efficiently sorting the wheat from the chaff. The genuinely sick people were hanging in there, but the others bolted and so they should. If man-tears were worse than your symptoms, then you hadn't needed to come to Emergency in the first place, and at the rate he was going Louis would have the department cleaned out before eight am.

As I mentioned earlier, Louis could be mean sometimes.

'I have a shooting pain down my left arm, radiating into my chest!' Louis bleated on this particular day. He had his heart attack symptoms slightly back to front and it was almost a shame, after his swotting, that he wasn't actually having one. He *really* wanted to be admitted to hospital but the doctors would not play ball.

Louis's constant presence at the hospital was a given but even by his lofty standards, shit was getting ridiculous. This was the fourth time he had called an ambulance to drive him the six blocks from his accommodation to triage *this morning*, and it wasn't yet ten thirty. Everyone was getting pissed off now, not least Louis himself because the doctors were refusing to review him again as his test results and observations were completely normal. He'd had an electrocardiogram and bloods taken, and both had returned 'NAD' – 'No Abnormalities Detected' – which probably wasn't something Louis heard very often. This time around, the only thing wrong with Louis was that there was nothing physically wrong with him, and he so desperately wanted there to be.

'I'M IN TERRIBLE PAIN!' he bellowed at the admitting clerk who had asked what was wrong so she could enter him on the database. *Again*. 'I AM HAVING A HEART ATTACK!'

'I'm warning you, Louis! There's no need to raise your voice!' the nurse in charge admonished him, but Louis was not in the mood for a reprimand, or to comply with requests. He was just incensed that he wasn't being strapped to a trolley and immediately rushed off to Cardiology or Intensive Care.

'I'M IN TERRIBLE PAIN AND YOU ARE NOT DOING ANYTHING ABOUT IT, YOU FUCKING HORRIBLE PEOPLE!'

'*Louis!*' The nurse glared at him and he rounded on her.

'I'M GOING TO FUCK YOU!' he roared. 'AND NOT IN THE CLASSICAL WAY!'

The nurse was horrified, and called security, and I had to walk away hurriedly before I burst out laughing.

Louis may have been a lot of things, but tenacious was

top of the list. The next day he was back, and I overheard him explaining why to the triage nurse. Apparently he had just consumed six litres of Diet Coke, and now he had a pain in his stomach.

'It's my appendix!' he said, urgently. 'You need to take it out before it BURSTS!'

The first time I laid eyes on Jeanette, I was actually at the supermarket, daydreaming, as a guy with an 'Elvis' name badge scanned my groceries. I saw a very angry-looking woman storm up to the cigarette counter at the front of Coles, grab the microphone they use for price checks and unleash a torrent of passionate yet largely incomprehensible abuse. I caught a couple of 'fucks' but not much else. Everybody in the supermarket froze. She wrapped up her brief tirade, turned around and stomped off, looking just as pissed off as she had before she vented, so it unfortunately didn't seem to have been very cathartic. She was wearing a green pyjama top I recognised from the hospital, and a long skirt that ended mid calf, mismatched socks and sneakers. She had obviously been a Mental Health patient at some point, and probably needed to be one again fairly soon.

It was a surreal moment, and everybody kind of looked at one another and shrugged, like, 'Did that really just happen?' then went back to leafing through magazines they were never going to buy. Elvis didn't miss a beat. He was a machine.

The second time I saw Jeanette, she was being dragged into Emergency – kicking and screaming, spitting and biting – by four cops. They got her to a bay and pushed her onto the bed, and told her they would take the handcuffs off if she calmed down, which she evidently had no intention of doing. She had green paint all over her face and in her hair and down her shirt, like real life modern art. She had been drinking it, trying to kill herself.

'Fuck you!' she screamed repeatedly. 'Fuck you, pigs! Fuck you!'

The third time, she had just been found licking blood off the floor in the Emergency waiting room, and it wasn't her blood. After that, I lost count.

I was actually afraid of Jeanette, which was unusual. I crossed paths with hostile bodies quite often, and some patients could be intimidating or difficult to subdue when they were blowing off steam, but at least you knew where you stood with them. They hated you, and you knew they hated you. There was a clear demarcation. They were the reason that big posters saying 'PHYSICAL OR VERBAL ABUSE IS <u>NOT</u> ACCEPTABLE!' were plastered all over the hospital. But Jeanette was different. She was the reason there was a mandatory three-day self-defence training course, with a one-day refresher every year. She was the kind of person who would hand you a teddy bear and a bunch of flowers to get you off guard then stab you in the face with a broken bottle because you didn't say 'bless you' when she'd sneezed three weeks earlier. She stopped at unpredictable just to fill up her tank, and didn't stop again until she hit buck wild and volatile, or a few policemen, whichever came first.

Luckily for me, Jeanette didn't think she had a drug problem, despite all the evidence to the contrary, so she never wanted to talk to me, and you couldn't help someone who didn't want to be helped. That was the beautiful thing about my job, and also the reason it could be so frustrating and most days felt like you were pissing up a rope.

'My only fucken drug problem is when I run out!' Jeanette said with a spiteful laugh, the first, last and *only* time I ever attempted to speak to her about her substance use. I steered clear of her in a professional capacity after that, but saw her frequently in Emergency. She always put on quite a show, compelling like a car crash.

Jeanette was fond of both alcohol and amphetamines, neither of which gelled particularly well with her assorted psychiatric diagnoses, and muddied the waters of effective treatment to the point of sludge. The amphetamines seemed to most dramatically disrupt her mental state and turned her speech to poisonous gibberish, like she was speaking in tongues. She would stand and rant, shaking her handcuffed wrists at the ceiling or God or whatever was above her, surrounded by bored policemen who watched her with wholly blank expressions and discussed whether they should get dinner from Hungry Jack's or McDonald's later on, with the occasional aside to Jeanette to 'pipe down'. I felt sorry for the police. If the psychiatric unit was busy they could be stuck there for hours, dispassionate babysitters to a charge who never shut up and didn't have a nice word to say to anyone.

I'm not sure which substance option I liked least for Jeanette, because she was a total nightmare on both of her favourites. Amphetamines made her seem possessed, and alcohol made her messy, emotional and loud. You'd hear her coming long before you saw her, even from inside a police car with all the windows wound up and through two sets of automatic doors.

'Stop hitting me! OW! Somebody help me! I'm being assaulted!' she screamed at the top of her lungs, although the police were trying to keep as much distance as possible between themselves and her to avoid being spat on, scratched, bitten or accused of brutality. She was infamous for filing complaints, lurid claims of being beaten and raped in custody, and had been known to throw herself down flights of stairs to intentionally cause a catalogue of nasty injuries to substantiate her allegations. Girlfriend was hardcore.

When Jeanette was being an arsehole, wishing people AIDS and calling them names and threatening to stab them with a used syringe, it was hard to find much kindness and empathy for her, but there *was* actually a person beneath the behaviour, and her life had been pure shit from the get-go. She'd had what is known as a 'prejudicial childhood', which in her case meant being physically abused from six months of age and bashed forever after for any and every misstep, no matter how slight. The sexual abuse started when she was seven.

When she was finally removed from the family home and put into Catholic 'care', the spectrum of abuse just grew wider, and there was nowhere left for her to go. She ran away and lived on the streets, found comfort in substances via prostitution, which was hardly salvation, and had been on the merry-go-round of hospital, jail and overdoses since before her 14th birthday. If life was fair you would only hate the behaviour – the game and not the player – but Jeanette made that difficult. Nobody could see what had happened to her *before*, but they could clearly see what was happening in the present moment, and it usually wasn't terribly endearing. Jeanette's public relations assault might have been more effective if it hadn't been so closely aligned with actual assault, but I wasn't about to enlighten her. It would have ended in tears, and me swallowing my own teeth – and that was probably an overly optimistic scenario.

Depending on how volcanic she was when she was brought into hospital, Jeanette was physically and chemically restrained, pinned down by nurses and security guards and knocked out with sedatives and anti-psychotics to smother the fury. She fought it, screaming and snarling, until her eyes rolled back in her skull, and then she finally slumped. She almost looked peaceful when she was unconscious – almost – but the embers still burnt, red-hot and incandescent, underneath the surface. Jeanette might go out for a while, but it was never over with her. She always came back blazing, like an angry meteor burning up on re-entry.

Jeanette had a smorgasbord of afflictions to choose from, but one of the more notable was trichotillomania, or compulsively pulling out your hair. There was a permanent bald spot on the left side of her head where she wrenched out handfuls of hair and sometimes chunks of skin. When she was stressed, you could tell just by looking at her scalp, although the ruckus that came with it somewhat spoiled the surprise.

'There's nothing wrong with me! Birds do this! And monkeys!' Jeanette shrieked at the paramedics as she tore out a bunch of her hair by the roots. It was true, feather plucking is a form of self-mutilation for captive birds, and some require anti-depressants or anti-psychotics to stop. The one thing you don't do, though, is yell at, or punish them for it, because it only teaches the bird that feather plucking will get them attention, and the same philosophy was applied to Jeanette. There's nothing to see here, nothing at all, just a psychotic woman partially scalping herself and screaming bloody murder.

In Emergency, when things got crazy, the craziness just kept coming. Full moons were the worst, and you didn't have to peer up into the night sky to know where in the lunar cycle we were because you could just sneak a peek at the waiting room. It was already chaos, bodies and trolleys everywhere, when I saw Jeanette march in the front door, spoiling for something. She had a cast on her right arm, and within five seconds was attempting to smash it to powder against the waiting room wall, screaming obscenities as she deftly re-fractured an already broken wrist, shattering bone fragments into splinters.

Somebody shouted, 'Get security!' and Jeanette just screamed louder, her tirade bouncing off the walls as parents clamped their hands over their kids' ears and told them not to look at her and old ladies shook their heads in disgust. I headed for the safety of my office, locked the door behind me, and watched as the hulking silhouettes of the security guards passed by like an eclipse.

The next morning Jeanette was prowling around the psychiatric clearing centre with a face like thunder and a brand-new cast on her arm, and there was a request for a 'drug and alcohol review' in her chart. I stuck my head out the door of the glass cubicle where the nurses worked, and called out her name.

'Excuse me, Jeanette?'

She looked up sharply, like a mean guard dog spying an intruder.

'Would you maybe like to talk about your drug and alcohol use with me for a few minutes?' I asked her, feeling nervous.

She stared at me, venomously, for five quite uncomfortable seconds.

'*Fuck* off!' she said.

'Rightio,' I said, shutting the door and returning to write in her chart *Patient declined drug and alcohol input*, which was a polite understatement.

About six months after I left my job in Emergency, I crossed paths with Jeanette again. I recognised her immediately, although she looked very different, standing on a street corner selling *The Big Issue* magazine and smiling at people.

I bought a copy.

Bill

Some drunks are hard to like, but Bill was one of my favourites. He was of Welsh descent, 47 years old and an alcoholic, and had been visiting the hospital on a semi-regular basis for about five years. Most times he was brought in by an ambulance, unconscious, after being scraped off the footpath, or being found passed out in a car park somewhere. Sometimes he just wandered in off the street and stood swaying at the front desk, smiling moronically, too drunk to speak, or he fell asleep in a chair in the waiting room and snored at industrial volume. He tended to go on wild benders, ending up in Emergency every day for a week, and then abruptly disappearing again. After a few weeks, just when you thought, *Gosh, I haven't seen Bill in, like, forever* . . . he would turn up, steaming and stinking, with new cuts and bruises and broken teeth, or a black eye, or coughing up blood, and the cycle began anew.

Sober, he was almost unrecognisable. First there was the element of surprise that he *was* sober, and then there was

the startling absence of drool, vomit, piss-stained clothing, matted hair and caked-on dirt, replaced instead by a
clean-shaven face and the knowledge that Bill did in fact
have access to running water and soap, at least some of the
time. When he tried, he was actually quite well turned
out, almost distinguished with slightly greying hair, and
perfectly pleasant and polite. But you only had to add alcohol and a bit of recreational speed and, hey presto, he was
a spectacular fuckup again.

When I saw Bill sober, which was admittedly rarely,
I would say hello and he'd look at me with a quizzical
expression, and genuinely have no idea who I was or
how it had come to pass that I knew his name, despite
the hospital ID hanging around my neck with the words
DRUG & ALCOHOL SERVICE written on it. Occasionally he gave me this semi-lascivious look, like he was
trying to remember if he knew me from having hooked
up at some point, which was disturbing. The 50 times we
had crossed paths in hospital previously were seemingly
wiped clean from the slate, like a lot of his other grog-
soaked memories, no doubt, and probably the majority
of his brain cells as well. He was heading down the road
to Korsakoff's, a psychosis from drinking that's basically
an alcohol-induced dementia, at a rate of knots. When
he performed poorly on a mental-state examination yet
again, one of the nurses said, 'Well, at least he can hide
his own Easter eggs this year.'

So there was an upside to irreversible brain damage
after all.

Bill was wasted, again, and bailing up a doctor in the corridor. He was wearing one of those hunting caps with fluffy earflaps, a filthy t-shirt, shorts and thongs, and looked like the guy who shot John Lennon, only older and drunker. His feet were so dirty they were black, and he smelt strongly of bitter, acrid sweat, even at a distance.

'Yeah, okay, no more hugs, thanks Bill,' the doctor said sternly, holding his arms out to fend off another attempted embrace. Bill could be very handsy and big on public displays of affection at times. He had a lot of love to give, but not many takers.

'I love ya, Doc!' Bill blurted.

'Uh huh. Thanks, Bill. You can go when you've had something to eat.' The doctor turned and started walking away.

'WHAT TIME IS IT, DOC?' Bill bellowed after him.

'Nine thirty!' the doctor called out over his shoulder without looking back, then added: 'IN THE MORNING.'

Bill fell into one of the green recliner chairs and fumbled with his plastic lunchbox of snacks, pulled a sandwich quarter out, stuffed it all in his mouth and chewed messily as he sat there grinning like a winner. He was a happy drunk this morning, which was way better than when he was a nasty drunk. It was an ongoing mystery; hugs, punches, kisses or kicks, you never knew which touching forget-me-not you were going to get from Bill. It was one of the most exciting things about him.

I sat down in the chair next to him. He smiled and exuberantly shook my hand like it was a snake he was trying to stun and I took it back, with just a little effort.

'Hey, Bill, how are things?' I asked. My guess was about 0.35 – he was wankered.

He beamed at me and swallowed his mouthful of half-chewed sandwich like a seagull gulping a hot chip at the beach. It looked like it barely touched his throat, just dropped straight down into his stomach.

'I'm engaged . . . to be *maaarried*!' he said sloppily. 'My bride-to-be, she's *beauuutiful*!'

'Really? Wow.' I was surprised. 'Congratulations.'

Supposedly there's someone for everyone, but Bill seemed to be kicking the piss out of that romantic ideal in a major way. The lucky lady must have been seriously hard-pressed for a date. I guessed she was either a fellow boozer, or mentally unsound.

'Does your, um, fiancée, drink, too?' I asked.

He gorged on another chunk of bread, then shook his finger at me as he chewed and swallowed.

'She's a . . . Christian,' he explained. 'God saved her . . . and she says He can save me, too.'

Of course she was a Christian.

He hiccuped loudly.

'Well, what does she think about your drinking?' I asked, and he blithely ignored me and began rambling on about how he had gotten into a fight with a gang of bikies recently: 'The bastards were out tha fron of the church . . . and I said, "I'll take ya! I'll take *all-a ya*!"'

The booze vapours coming off him suddenly overpowered me, making me feel nauseous. It was a little too early in the morning for his furious second-hand ethanol.

184

'*Jesus*, Bill!' I gasped, taking his fiancée's god's name in vain. 'How much have you had to drink this morning?'

He continued to ignore me, then launched into a new, ponderous story with so many narrative twists, turns and somersaults that I listened, bemused, for a few minutes and realised that the more he said, the less I understood, which seemed almost artful. On the other hand, he left me no alternative; I was going to have to enter the conversation by force. After all, I was supposed to be performing some kind of 'therapeutic intervention' here, not just listening to him talk shit endlessly.

'Bill, what about your drinking?' I interrupted him. 'What's the plan with that?'

He already had a busted liver, a faltering pancreas, hepatitis C and numerous other ailments, all partially related to, or accelerated by, the five litres of Fruity Lexia he consumed on an average day. The wine was so sweet, it was amazing he didn't have diabetes already, but that was certainly something else he had to look forward to in the future, besides his upcoming nuptials. He stopped talking, which I considered some small degree of progress. Then he looked at me and smiled, channelled Rod Stewart and began singing 'I Don't Want To Talk About It'.

I burst out laughing, which was just the encouragement he *didn't* need.

'Cut it out, Bill!' I said, trying to get my face on straight, but it was hilarious and, drunk as he was, we both knew my credibility was shot. 'Come on, Bill,' I pleaded, 'you're in hospital, not at karaoke. Shut up!' But his smile just widened and he closed his eyes so he could really get into it. His singing voice was pretty decent, but extremely loud, and everyone was turning around to look at us. Bill didn't give a shit, but I was squirming. I put my pen back in my pocket and shut my folder.

'Okay, I'm out of here,' I said, standing up, and Bill serenaded me all the way down the corridor and, even when I couldn't see him anymore, I could still hear him. But, you know, it could have been much worse, and the next month it was.

Bill was having his head sutured again, for the second time in a week. The first lot of stitches were put in when he had fallen over pissed, *quelle surprise*, and smacked his head on the gutter. The divorced hemispheres of his lacerated scalp were reunited, Panadol administered for his headache, and he had sobered up enough to manage the walk back to the bottle shop around the corner, so he went and got bladdered again. As you do.

A few days after that he had split his sutures open during a fight in the park, when a homeless guy had tried to take off with the last of his goon and Bill had stopped him. He had chugged what was left of his cask, and then wandered into hospital when he realised he was bleeding.

'That's the lowest, *lowest* dog act of all!' Bill had said, with passionate, pissed indignation, when the doctor asked him what he'd been fighting about. 'You can fuck my woman, or steal my wallet, or *whatever*, I don't *care*, but you never . . . you *never* take another man's drink!' Bill attempted to shake his head, further conveying his disgust.

'Keep your head still!' the doctor snapped at him. 'I'm almost finished.'

'*Ohhh*, sorry, Doc!' Bill giggled. 'Sorry, maaate!'

'Okay, we're done.' The doctor snipped the last bit of nylon thread with his scissors, after adding another four stitches to the five Bill already had, and Bill got up off the trolley.

'Thanks, Doc! You're a fucken staaar!' he said merrily, clearly unsteady on his feet but nonetheless preparing to hit the road. The doctor bundled up his suture kit and turned his back to write in the chart, while Bill waved away the nurse who was trying to get him to sit back down. I watched uneasily from the counter, where I was writing up another patient's notes. Bill was going to get ornery in a minute. While he was undoubtedly drunk, he wasn't drunk enough to do what he was told, and he had a problem listening to the sensible reasoning of others on a good day. I had a strong sense of foreboding.

'I'm *fiiiine!*' he told the nurse, shrugging off the steadying arm she offered him.

'You're drunk,' she said. 'And you're covered in blood. Why don't you sit back down for a minute? I'll get you something to eat. And a coffee.'

'*Naaah*, luv! 'Sall good!' he said and tried to wink at her but it just came out looking like he had some kind of palsy. He patted his shirt pocket to make sure his pouch of tobacco was where he had left it, and as if trying to prove how sober, coordinated and in control he was, Bill took three overly confident steps away from the bed. Before you could say 'timber', he had fallen straight backwards. It all happened so quickly, nobody could do anything except gasp.

As his skull smashed into the linoleum floor, there was a sickeningly dull *thud*, the way I imagine a wet piñata dropped from a great height would sound. His eyelids fluttered rapidly, then shut, and a pool of blood quickly appeared around his head in a grisly halo. It was as if time stopped: there was a tiny yet absolute pause, and then people suddenly came flying from every direction in a flurry of activity. I felt faint.

'That stupid motherfucker,' I said, to no one in particular. I looked across at the doctor, who had turned his back for no more than 20 seconds, only to find Bill spreadeagled and bleeding on the ground, and all his handiwork in ruins, yet again.

He looked at the carnage in front of him and sighed. You could tell he really meant it.

Bill vanished from the hospital after that last head injury, and I never saw him again. I liked to imagine that he had gone on an endless round-the-world honeymoon with his new wife and that they were in Italy eating spaghetti and meatballs from the same plate, just like Lady and the Tramp.

Jacinta

I would walk to my office in the morning via the waiting room in Emergency and my little cherubs, the drug and alcohol patients, stuck out like sore thumbs. And by sore thumbs, I don't mean a thumb accidentally tapped with a hammer while undertaking some gentle DIY, I mean a thumb mashed like a potato. My patients were the ones causing a fuss, asleep on the floor, yelling, crying, or vomiting into a bag or a bin. They weren't *all* hell on wheels, some people did just sit quietly and wait for their name to be called without causing a ruckus, but it was not uncommon for them to act like jackasses. It was kind of their 'thing'.

Jacinta was the first cab off the rank this morning, and to call her a bag of bones did her no justice at all. She was stoned and swaying on her feet, all drowsiness and repetitive movement with one properly gimpy leg, and looked like she weighed about 40 kilograms. She was a junkie with cancer, suck *squared*, and had turned up requesting a 'drug and alcohol review', but that was as much as I knew.

The previous chart entries said that Jacinta had fallen down two flights of stairs at the train station on Christmas Day and that she had ended up in hospital for a week of further investigation because her routine blood tests had come back completely deranged. And now I was trying to fathom Jacinta's scattered thought process enough to write comprehensible admission notes. I needed to find out why she was here and what she wanted. It felt like pushing shit uphill, and really heavy giant boulder-type shit at that.

'*So*, I've got *lymphomaaa*,' she said dopily, 'and my oncologist wants me to fucken *detox*, just because I've been an IVF drug user.'

I was pretty sure she meant she had been an intravenous drug user, and not an in-vitro fertilisation drug user. And I was surer still that the use of past tense when discussing her drug use was inappropriate, as she was very much wasted in the present.

'You'll have to excuse *meee*,' she drawled, 'but I was in such a hurry to get here that I forgot to put underwear *onnn*.'

Too wasted to remember to put on underpants before leaving the house, in fact. Well, that was a new one. Jacinta was fidgety and restless as a monkey, constantly repositioning herself, crossing and uncrossing her legs and smoothing her dress over her knees to protect her modesty. Her fingers were stained dark orange from smoking and her teeth were a mess, all broken, jagged little points on the bottom, and brown and crumbling. She had false teeth that she wore sometimes, she said, but they didn't fit that well because they had belonged to her ex-boyfriend, before he overdosed and died. That was two boyfriends ago. The one *after* him was in jail for armed robbery, and the one after *him* had kicked it with an overdose, too.

'I've been a bit unlucky in love,' Jacinta said.

The steroids Jacinta had been having as part of her cancer treatment had made her really hungry, so she was simultaneously drinking a coffee and a chocolate Big M and eating spoonfuls of yoghurt while she droned on and on. She brought the coffee cup to her lips and, just as she was about to take a sip, she thought of something else to say and put the cup down again, then distractedly picked up the Big M instead. I made a game, like a horse race, of guessing what she was going to put in her mouth next. Would she *finally* take a drink of the chocolate milk, or would the coffee come from behind and stage an upset? The Big M straw was at her mouth, it looked like it was going to happen . . . but *no*! She put the milk carton down and the *yoghurt* took the lead. It was anybody's race! This was much more fun than trying to follow the ponderous verbal ramble she was weaving around me.

Wants to detox from . . . was all I had written on her chart. She had obviously been using opiates in the last couple of hours, because she was dumb as a rock and her pupils were practically invisible, but she wasn't giving me any information that was remotely helpful or instructive. No, Jacinta was only interested in telling me about her South American parakeet, Chuck, and how he had kept her company the last time she had gotten clean at home.

Jacinta said that one day she just decided that she was sick of the shit (prostitution) to put shit (heroin) up her arms, only to end up feeling like shit (withdrawal) all over again so she had taken matters into her own hands. Taking matters into her own hands meant Jacinta had spent her drug money on a parakeet from a pet shop. He was going to act as her companion while she went cold turkey, because all the humans she knew were users, too, and she was allergic to dogs, cats, rabbits and guinea pigs. She constructed an aviary inside her kitchen and covered Chuck's cage with flowers to mimic a jungle canopy so he felt more at home, because he was an import and not a native Australian bird and 'didn't speak the language of the other birds around'. Chuck would sit on her shoulder while she watched TV, creep up to her face and pry open her mouth with his beak, sampling everything she ate directly from her mouth. It didn't sound very hygienic to me. Jacinta had also built a perch for him in her bedroom, right into the headboard of her bed. The only problem with Chuck was that he would squirt shit all over the place, like in her bed, and on the floor, and sometimes *in her hair when she was sleeping.* I grimaced. Her place sounded like a hellhole to me, a stinking, crap-covered, life-sized birdcage. Jacinta had been wondering if it would be possible to toilet-train him, because he was a super-smart bird, but then her boyfriend had left the window open one afternoon, and Chuck had flown off into the ether, never to be seen again. Jacinta was so bummed she went out and scored.

Her terrific limp was collateral damage from the heroin binge that followed Chuck's defection. She had fallen unconscious with a leg buckled and bent beneath her and sustained permanent nerve damage, a condition known as compartment syndrome. It had left her hobbling like a pirate with a wooden leg. All she needed was an eye patch and for Chuck to fly back into her life, and her Halloween costume was sorted for the rest of her life. And looking at the state of her, that probably wasn't going to be very long.

I don't know why junkies spoke the way they did, but they had this whiny, drawn out speech that was exhausting to listen to. They were a 45 record playing at 33⅓, and it was *painful*. Jacinta was on a bucketload of pills, as well as the heroin, and just when I thought she was going to nod off and her speech petered out, she had a sudden burst of energy, revived and resumed her monotonous diatribe. It was never going to end. I sat and stared at her, and she talked and talked and *talked*. Then her speech slowed, her head began to droop again, and her neck bent like a palm tree in a cyclone . . . It was like watching someone fall asleep, but never quite making it there, and talking all the while.

'My brother used to bash me, and rape *meeee*,' she slurred. 'My whole family are fucken *bastards*!'

A sketchy-looking guy tapped on the glass of the waiting room window, raised his eyebrows questioningly, and Jacinta gave him a wave.

'That's my boyfriend, Jason,' she told me. 'He really looks after *meee*.'

'Does he use, too?' I asked, although I didn't need to. He just had 'the look', like he would hock his mother at Cash Converters without blinking and then lose the receipt he needed to claim her back. Perhaps it was overly harsh, but he looked like a dirtbag.

'*Yeaah*, but we've both *reeally* cut back since the O*Deee* . . .'

Jacinta was in a coma just five days ago, as it turned out. She had slid easily into respiratory arrest after a hit and lay on a trolley in the resuscitation bay like a side of beef, a tube down her throat and a machine pushing air into her lungs. The Narcan infusion soaked into her system, slowly washing the junk off her opiate receptors and bringing her back to life.

Jason had come storming in when he found out what had happened, and he let his intubated and ventilated limp lettuce leaf of a girlfriend really have it.

'You fucken *bitch*! You were supposed to score for *both of us*! Where's my fucken gear? I can't believe you shot up *all my fucken gear*! You took it all, YOU FUCKEN BITCH!'

Everybody was impressed by his compassionate, caring attitude. It was another beautiful opiate love story, a romantic fairytale for the ages.

The romanticisation of heroin by the fashion industry during its short-lived early-nineties flirtation was poetic licence at its zenith. 'Heroin chic' was an oxymoron. It was a terribly aging, complexion-ruining, car crash of a drug. There was nothing chic about it, although it did bring out your cheekbones, and your collarbone, and all of your other bones, too. It was great for weight loss and as a Harry Potter-style invisibility potion, because it made everything disappear. Like your family, your money, your looks, your health, your dignity and your ability to answer in the negative if someone asked you if you had hepatitis C or HIV. It was an awesome destroyer of worlds.

Most of Jacinta's veins had collapsed. Now she injected into her neck and groin because those were the only veins that still worked. She was 39 but looked 59, although if you closed your eyes you could have sworn you were listening to a really flaky teenager. She had five kids, and two grandkids, and none of them were going to see her make old bones.

It was a shame Jacinta had found refuge in narcotics, because now she had cancer, there wasn't really anywhere for her to go for pain relief because her neural circuit board was trashed and worn out. She was going to get her drugs for free in the Oncology ward, but it would be in negligible amounts compared to what she was used to. When she couldn't get any heroin, Jacinta had been using 300mg of morphine a day, and anything less than that was going to feel like pissing in the wind to her. Hospital was going to be a bumpy ride.

Junkies were the one group of patients who didn't get a lot of sympathy in hospital. The attitude that substance abuse was self-inflicted and not a *real* disease compared to things like cancer and diabetes was fairly widespread and some nurses could be mercenary and punitive when it came to dishing out analgesia to people with a history of intravenous drug use. Some liked their patients a little more vanilla and a lot less rocky road, and Jacinta's life was nothing *but* rocky road. The way I looked at it, you made a really dumb decision once upon a time, and then you had to live with it for the rest of your life. It was hard *not* to feel sorry for people who had opened that particularly rotten can of worms, and then had to go opiate fishing for the rest of their days. Heroin was a shitty crush to have. You could love it with all your heart, and people did, but it was never going to love you back.

Rochelle

When I was working in Emergency on the weekends, I had my usual quota of PFD (Pissed and Fallen Down) patients and nightclub overdosers to visit, and I also doubled as the on-call drug and alcohol nurse for the rest of the hospital. There were frequent phone calls asking for a review of patients who had issues with substances, and even more problematic personalities that the regular nurses weren't quite sure how to deal with. Sometimes a patient had disclosed, during a routine admission for an otherwise unrelated condition, that they had a history of intravenous drug use, and even if they had been clean for 20 years, it was usually enough to get a panicked phone call from a spooked nurse who felt that even long-term ex-junkies extended well beyond their clinical comfort zone. Other times the patients were extremely current drug and alcohol patients, who kept leaving the ward for 'a cigarette' and came back drunk or on the nod, or continually pestered the nurses for Valium and painkillers because they were 'in withdrawal'. So there was often a legitimate reason for me to show up and review people, if only to tell the nurses that, yes, this patient *was* taking the piss and was not in any kind of perilous, life-threatening withdrawal. Other times I just shot the breeze for a while, chatting to patients who had their substance use under control, and did nothing more strenuous than hand out a couple of pamphlets.

Rochelle was last on my list of outlying patients to see. She was in the Maxillofacial Unit, my old student stomping ground, waiting to have a skin graft to cover the deep, jagged lacerations on her face. She had shot up some heroin in her kitchen for the first time in a few weeks, and as she was rinsing the syringe barrel out with hot water, she went on the nod and fell face-forward onto a pile of glasses and plates, at just the right angle and level of force so they shattered. The real estate people had turned up for a housing inspection and found her in a pool of blood on the kitchen floor with a discarded spoon and syringe beside her and half her face chopped up like beef strips for a stir-fry. As far as rental property inspections go, it wasn't the best day for Century 21 real estate, but it could perhaps be seen as a mean-spirited victory for resentful renters everywhere.

The other nurses gave me a warm welcome when I turned up late in the evening.

'She's in that room over there.' They pointed. 'Good luck!'

Their cynical well wishes didn't fill me with confidence.

I knocked on the door, and a girl with a bandage wrapped around most of her head like a mummy, who was quite small and looked about 16 and like she wouldn't hurt a fly, glanced at me with her uncovered eye. When I told her I was from the drug and alcohol service, she smiled. The patients were often just as happy to see me as the other nurses, at first, because they thought I would increase their pain relief to the habit levels they were accustomed to. When the penny finally dropped, and they realised I wasn't going to do their bidding, the friendliness usually stopped, too.

Rochelle said she had a 'split personality', and that's why she was always waking up in jail, getting into trouble and, most unfairly, having to deal with consequences that were not of her making. She felt very hard done by.

'It's not me! I mean, it *is* me, but it's not *me*! The *other* me beats people up with a baseball bat, and then *I* get in trouble for it! I'm sick of waking up in the watch house with the pigs telling me all the shit I'm *supposed* to have done!'

Apparently her other personality was a real arsehole.

Rochelle started to cry, and I got her a box of tissues. She told me the long, winding story of her life and there was not one single bright or cheerful spot, at least not the way she told it. Even her *own mother* had never been particularly sympathetic to her plight. Rochelle had been staying with her for the very few days she had spent out of hospital since she chop-sueyed her face, having lost her accommodation, but it was falling far short of her expectations.

'I'll be in bed at nine o'clock, in a deep sleep, and she comes *storming* into my room, yelling, "Get up! Have a shower! Out of bed *now*!"' Her good eye filled to the brim and more tears slid down her face. 'And I need someone to say, "Okay, Rochelle, time to wake up now!"' She pretended to gently rouse someone from slumber, easing them into consciousness with the lightness of a feather.

I was beginning to feel pretty sorry for Rochelle. She had no insight or sense of personal responsibility, an addictive personality mixed with a violent streak a mile wide, and now a severely munted profile as well. And then she excused herself to answer a call on her mobile phone.

'Yeah, hi, Dad . . . Yeah, those fucken cunt nurses won't give me any decent pain relief! They give me *one Endone*, and Endone's like eating a fucken *Smartie* after having a habit! They won't let me smoke inside so I have to go outside in the fucken *street* . . .' Her vitriol spewed wild and free. She was going to 'punch the bitch out' if the nurses gave her any grief tonight. It looked like her 'other personality' had come to visit, and she was a piece of work.

Rochelle complained about the room she was in and had pulled the curtains shut around her bed to isolate herself, which was more of a gift to her roommates than a well-executed act of antisocial aggression. Profound deafness would have been an excellent gift for them, too.

'Between *his* farting, and *his* fucken TV being on all night and *her* bullshit,' she motioned at the other occupants of the room, 'I can't fucken *stand it*! I want my *own* bed, and my cat, and some DECENT fucken drugs! This doesn't exactly fucken tickle, you know!' She pointed at her face.

It was becoming increasingly easy for me to picture her brandishing a baseball bat in a non-athletic fashion. And then five seconds later she visibly deflated, her anger fell in on itself like a crumpled parachute, and she started to tear up again. She was all over the place.

'I've been awake for three days,' Rochelle said, sniffing, and perhaps explaining why her one visible pupil was as big as a saucer, blacking out her entire iris except for a very thin ring of colour, a hint of blue around the edge.

'Well, it's pretty hard to feel good and think rationally when you're that sleep-deprived. And things always seem worse at night,' I said gently, trying to reassure her but she wouldn't budge.

'Yeah, but the thing is, when I sleep, I *dream*. And I dream about finding my family impaled on star pickets, or being locked in a concrete room full of blood. And I'm *drowning*. In *blood*,' she said, with a certain amount of relish in her voice, like she was even a little fond of her tortured existence and the inner turmoil expressed as night terrors.

'*Riiight* . . . well, maybe sleep isn't the answer then . . .' I replied. 'Um, do you eat?'

She was thin, but didn't seem obviously malnourished.

'I eat every three days, milk or yoghurt only. And water,' she said, defiantly.

'What about fruit and vegetables?'

'Ugh, gross! They make me *gag*!' And she made a face like she wanted to vomit.

'Okay, well, how many cigarettes do you smoke a day?'

'Fifty. White Ox rollies, you know, the real strong shit.'

I sighed. I suddenly felt tired, and realised I was in the presence of an expert psychic vampire. She was looking brighter and I was drained and only sliding further into the funk of not giving a shit.

'So, let me get this straight,' I said. 'You shoot up heroin, you starve yourself for days at a time, then eat only dairy products . . . you sometimes stay up for half a week, and you smoke about 50 cigarettes a day . . .'

'Yep.'

'Right,' I said. 'Do you take a multivitamin or anything like that?'

'No way, that shit gives you cancer! I saw it on *A Current Affair*!'

I was torn between wanting to laugh and wanting to slap the uninjured side of her face. Rochelle was an idiot. I looked at my watch.

'Okay, Rochelle, I really have to get going, but the thing is, you kind of have to start caring about what happens to you. Until then—'

'People *find* me!' she protested. 'I move to a new town, and before I know it, I'm stuck in the same situation there, too! People buying me drinks at the pub, then we all go back to their place and people start bringing out ice pipes and gear . . .'

In short, Rochelle was a furious shit magnet. Like attracts like.

Rochelle was appreciative of my time, and assured me that she didn't lump me in with the rest of the 'bitch nurses', but it didn't feel like I had actually done anything to help. Any advice or information I had given to her had bounced off her thick skull like water on an umbrella, and I had nothing to show for our interaction except fatigue. It was another sterling day at the office, but you don't work in drug and alcohol for the instant gratification, because there isn't any. The best you can hope for is that you never see the person again, because that means they might have gotten better. Or they might be in jail. Or they could be dead. I liked to tell myself that they were better. It made my job seem less redundant. It was in much the same way that I told myself that a patient I had just spent half an hour counselling must have *accidentally* dropped all the brochures and drug and alcohol information I had given them, and which I later found littered all over the footpath outside the hospital as I made my way home. Surely the patient hadn't just *thrown them away*, because that would mean I had wasted at least 30 minutes of my working day giving a shit. So I just told myself, repeatedly, that was not the case.

After my illuminating evening with Rochelle, I went home to my un-crazy family, to my mercifully drug- and drama-free home and ate takeaway Indian food with my visiting sister. By now, people were wary of asking about my day at work, because if I told them what I had actually seen or encountered, they were either sickened or appalled or clapped their hands to their mouths in amused horror. Still, curiosity usually got the better of them. When my younger sister, who had a non-mental job, asked how my day had been, I was so sick of the sound of my own voice after a day spent talking that I just said work had been fine and nothing much had happened. I ate naan and butter chicken and listened as my nine-year-old niece gave a couple of practice-runs of her oral presentation on the famous Australian Delta Goodrem for school the next day. Rochelle was gone, left back at the hospital, smoking cigarettes in the cold and scowling with the half of her face that still could, hating life, hating herself, hating everything.

Shane

Another day, and another drug overdose. That's just the way it went in Emergency. Whether it was intentional, as in attempted suicide, or recklessly careless, as in Amy Winehouse, there was usually somebody hooked up to an oxygen cylinder with a bloodstream full of kamikaze chemicals and their lips and fingertips turning blue. If there happened to be some decent heroin floating around the city that was higher in purity than usual – and there was really no way of knowing until it was too late – then junkies would sometimes be brought into Resus in pairs, like dysfunctional, drug-loving shoes that broke into houses a lot. They operated on a sort of 'buddy system' but it was a bit shit.

The Resuscitation area had four bays fitted with single beds and lots of monitors, highly equipped for those most at risk or in dire need of stabilisation, and next door to that was the Trauma room, where the motor-bike crashers and bodies extracted from mangled vehicles were housed. Not as many people died in Emergency as you might think; it was just the beginning of the line for most patients, unless they had fallen off a building or been consumed by a fireball. From Emergency, patients successfully kept alive were funnelled out to a satellite of other wards, like Intensive Care and the Burns Unit, and they usually bit the big one there instead. Resus was where the remainder ended up, people with serious conditions like failing lungs and cardiac problems, and the unconscious addicts, like Shane, who turned up to the hospital almost as regularly as I did.

Shane was on a trolley, sleeping sitting up. The paramedics had found him passed out in the street at the front of a methadone clinic with an empty blister pack of Xanax in his pocket and a fresh track mark in the crook of his left arm. He was covered in tattoos: a trail of tears down his face, black outlines with one coloured in red; *Marry* and *Me* tattooed on his eyelids; spider webs on his elbows and knees; and skulls, crosses and dragons everywhere else. He looked tough with all his jailhouse ink, but he was shorter than me, weighed about half as much and had long curly eyelashes like Bambi. His chart said he had just turned 24, and it was already three volumes thick. Diagnosis: *hot mess*.

Shane's oxygen levels were fluctuating, hovering at around 85%, but he was coming around slightly and kept pulling off his oxygen mask. You could tell when an overdoser was making their way back to the surface, because that was when they started becoming a total pain in the arse. They were too out of it to go home, but they weren't out of it enough to just do as they were told. They were annoyingly unmanageable, like my hair in a humid climate.

'SHANE! WHAT DID YOU TAKE? SHANE! WAKE UP! OPEN YOUR EYES!' the Emergency nurse yelled and shook his arm. This was the usual protocol for a drug overdose, and it was loud and persistent. The monitor clamped on his finger showed his oxygen levels were dropping in tandem with his nodding head.

Shane needed to wake up. The sooner he did, the sooner I could do my Drug and Alcohol thing and the sooner he could be kicked out of Emergency, simultaneously freeing up a bed and freeing me to pour another shitty hospital coffee down my neck. I knew that I needed an intervention where my caffeine intake was concerned, but I also knew that I was happily stuck at pre-contemplative on the 'stages of change' cycle, and would stab anyone who dared come between me and the next flat white. Shane and I were alike in that way: he had stabbed the last dealer who had ripped him off.

'BREATHE, Shane! Come on, take a few deep breaths!' the nurse hollered at him.

Shane opened his eyes eventually, when he had been poked, shaken and antagonised awake, and he began to respond to the constant questioning with more than just a mumbled bunch of incoherent bullshit. The nurse left me to work my 'magic'. Junkies were a hot potato that nobody else in Emergency wanted to catch.

'Wherami?' he slurred.

'You're in the hospital.'

'*Whaaa?*'

'What did you take today, Shane?'

Shane's heavy eyelids dropped, flashing *Marry Me, Marry Me* as he began to sink beneath the thin skin of consciousness again.

I poked him in the arm.

'Shane!'

'*What?*' He jolted awake and opened his eyes, looking both irritable and drowsy. Since he was found at the front of a methadone clinic, and its accompanying needle exchange service, with a needle mark in his arm, I thought I would begin my enquiries there.

'Have you used anything today, Shane?' I asked him, and the nature of my questioning was apparently so offensive that he immediately became more alert and coherent, which usually meant that I had hit the raw nerve welded to the truth, despite his vehement protest.

'I'm not a fucken *junkie*! Look at my teeth!' he said indignantly. 'I've got beautiful teeth, see?' He bared them at me like a horse waiting to be fed a sugar cube. 'I'm not a junkie! I'm not gonna ruin my *beautifuuul* teeth with *heroin* or fucken *methadone*!'

'Why do you have a needle mark in your arm? What's that from?' I asked.

'*Ohhh,* that's from jail,' he said, calming down, although he'd been out on parole for six weeks and this track mark was so new it was still spotted with blood and only just beginning to bruise.

'When did you last inject anything?' I asked him as his

eyelids fell, and half a marriage proposal fluttered in my direction. '*Shane!* When did you last inject?'

'I dunnooo . . .' He trailed off.

He denied that he used heroin, even though the 'friend' who had called the ambulance told them that he did, and I'd seen him in hospital with heroin overdoses on at least five previous occasions. Shane said that he had *only* taken all his Oxycontin – he was prescribed 80mg twice a day for 'back pain' – and seven or eight Xanax tablets, some Valium and a 'bit' of vodka. In other words, he had taken enough combined substances to kill himself three times, but some people just won't die, and it's not for lack of trying.

Ten minutes later, Shane had eaten three sandwiches, swallowed two containers of orange juice and was back on track, which is to say that he was talking shite and preparing to kick back into aggressive chemical-seeking mode, his natural state.

'I gotta go, I gotta seven-month-old baby and my girl's bringing the baby over, so I gotta get outta here,' he mumbled through heavily hooded lids while he attempted to undo the blood pressure cuff around his upper arm, with little success. It always amazed me how people with drug problems managed to reproduce so effectively between hits: DOCS babies had DOCS babies, who had DOCS babies . . .

'Hey, do you think I look better than last time you saw me?' Shane asked me.

'Uh, no.' Strangely enough, he looked like shit, like someone who had just overdosed.

'Nah, I know I'm under the influence an that, but do ya reckon I look better? I look healthier?'

He could barely hold his head up on his neck and really didn't care what I thought. Shane was just fishing for compliments, and if that's what it took to get him out of the bed, the Emergency Department and my hair, and not necessarily in that order, then so be it.

'Yeah, you look much better, Shane. You look *really* healthy,' I replied, dryly.

'Thanks, darl, I appreciate that. I feel better, eh.' He tried to wink at me, and it almost set him back on the nod.

A doctor passed by, glanced at the vital signs displayed on the monitor and said, 'He can go when he's awake,' then headed into the next bay where a man was quietly having a heart attack and Shane started slapping himself in the face.

'Wake up! *Wake up!*' he said, still slightly groggy.

I started sorting through his paperwork, preparing to write some rather unilluminating notes about Shane being a self-proclaimed abstainer from heroin and methadone and how his teeth were clearly a testament to this.

'Darl, *darl*!'

'That's not my name.'

'Aw, come on, *miiiiss*! I've got a brain injury! I can't remember names! What's your name, miss? Cos, miss, I need a script! I've only got four days left of Oxycontin so get the doctor to write *not to be used for four days*, like write the date four days from now, and I won't use them until then, but I'm running out of Oxy and you need to get me a new script,' Shane pleaded, droning like a drug-seeking robot.

'Well, that's not going to happen,' I told him. 'No' was not a word that addicts responded well to, as a rule, and Shane was just doing what he always did, and that was not listening. He was gifted in that way. I would go so far as to call him the best worst listener I had ever met.

'But I've got a letter from my doctor! It's in my chart, or in my pocket, or maybe somebody stole it . . . I just need more Oxy, and some Xanax! I'll have a fit, miss! Come on, *miiiss*!' he said.

'Shane, you just OD'd and you're still stoned. The doctor's not going to give you drugs to take home. You can wait and ask him yourself if you want.'

Shane obviously interpreted this as a physical challenge, got up off the trolley and started walking in a very crooked line, holding both arms straight out and away from his trunk.

'*See*, miss? I'm *fine*!' he said, wobbling over to the sink. 'I'm just going to splash some water on my face . . .' He turned on the hot water tap full bore.

'That water's going to get really hot in a second,' I warned him.

He held his hands under the tap, cupped them and threw the water in his face, left the tap running, then staggered back over to the trolley and sat down, dripping everywhere.

'I'm gonna go, miss, just call me a taxi, and listen, doc, I need some Oxycontin to take with me.'

'I'm not a doctor, Shane.'

'Miss, miss, but I need some Oxy! I just need some scripts, just look on the computer, you can see my history!'

he said, deaf to everything but his own monotonous voice and the urging of his habit.

'Sorry, Shane, I can't help you.'

'Miss! Miss! I just need a script! And I need another sandwich! I need a sandwich and some *Oxy*!' he called out as I walked away. I would write my notes later, for what they were worth. My desire for coffee trumped my interest in him by about a billion to one, and vice versa.

It was quite common for people to have seizures when they abruptly cut down on medications like Xanax and Valium. Shane was very mindful of this, having chipped one of his 'beautiful teeth' the last time he'd run out of Xanax and subsequently had a small fit. So when he was next arrested for possession and left stewing in a cell without his usual, heavily abused, medications, he elected to take the management of his anticipated withdrawal into his own hands.

First, he nagged and whined and begged for more medication than he had been given, which was not forthcoming, unsurprisingly. Next, he asked for a glass of water, which the police *were* willing to give to him, presenting it to him in a polystyrene cup. Shane drank the water, and then, logically, pulled down his pants, whizzed into the cup and *drank his own pee*. The police shook their heads in amused disgust. They'd seen this Bear Grylls-type shit before, except the last guy had squatted on the ground, contorted himself like a yogi and attempted to urinate directly into his mouth, which meant he had just ended up pissing in his own face.

'Youse made me do it! You're not giving me enough drugs!' Shane shouted. 'There's more Xanax in my fucking *piss* than what you're giving me!'

Obviously, when presented with the option of *potentially* having a seizure or drinking his own drug-soaked urine, Shane knew which side his bread was buttered on.

Don

It was another hectic day in Emergency, just for a change. One of the nurses, on her way to see a more critically ill patient, pointed at Don as I walked by and gave me a brutally succinct handover.

'Pissed, suicidal, psych are busy.' Which meant that Don was mine, all mine.

Don wanted to die, but first he was going to finish his egg sandwich. At least he had *something* to live for, even if it was only boiled egg that was in dire need of seasoning mashed between two slices of soggy white bread. He had the Emergency Department lunch special resting on his lap, a clear plastic box with a small container of orange juice and a tiny green apple still waiting to be consumed. I don't know why they bothered putting it in there; hardly anybody ate the fruit. It was probably some hospital-wide nutritional initiative, which was fine if people actually *ate* it, but most of the time they just pegged it into the bin.

Don smelt fresh, but not in a lovely, early morning dew or newly cut grass sort of way. He was giving off a deadly combination of body odour and metabolising alcohol as he sat in a green recliner in the corridor, but he did seem calm and relaxed, which was good. I took a quick look at his paperwork. He was *relaxed*, all right. He had relaxed his blood alcohol level all the way to 0.295.

'Don?' I asked, and the blond middle-aged man with an alarmingly red complexion and a bulbous nose peered up at me with eyes full of tears, chewing with his mouth open.

'You're Don?' I asked again. He nodded pitifully, and tears rolled down his cheeks. I pulled a chair up next to him and before I could introduce myself, or explain why I was there, Don swallowed the bolus of sandwich in his mouth and started spilling his guts.

'I've gotta plan,' he slurred, 'I'm gunna hang myself in my flat, I've dunnit before.' And he tilted his head back so I could see the torsion scar around his neck. 'It almost worked, too, but some *bastard* foun' me and cumme down! He had *no right*, NO RIGHT!'

Oh, dear. Don was in a bad way.

'Ya know why I wanna die?' he asked me, putting the half-eaten sandwich back in his lunch box so he could gift me with his full attention. Since I had been in his orbit for approximately 20 seconds, it was clearly a rhetorical question.

'No, why?'

'*Because* . . . I love women!' he proclaimed. 'But . . . *women* . . . don't love me *back*!'

'Oh,' I said. 'Right.' Frankly, I was disappointed. I thought it was going to be something a bit more dramatic than that. If unrequited love was justification enough for suicide, then I should have killed myself a hundred times already, starting when I was eight and Duran Duran didn't love me back. And Simon Le Bon was just the beginning, the tip of a fairly tragic romantic iceberg. I have a spectacular track record of wishful, one-sided love affairs that continues to this day (Hi Dan!). In my experience, when you accepted that your affection had ultimately amounted to being left stranded and alone in a cul-de-sac at the end of a one-way street, alcohol was the best remedy. The trick, though, was to drink until you found your happy place and set up camp there for a while, instead of drinking yourself to the unhappy, maudlin place that was the next stop down the line. Don needed to drink a little less and grow a pair. I did.

'No 'ffence, love,' Don said, conspiratorially, 'you're a woman, anna good lookin' one, but I *hate* WOMEN! Not you love, mind, well, not *yet*, but the women I've had, they've ruined my *fucken life*! Scuse my French . . .'

If *only* he were speaking in French. I wouldn't be able to understand a word he was saying *and* it would sound much nicer, because Don was never going to shut up. Drunk patients were the worst. They didn't know how to tell a short story, and they never started at the beginning, they started at the beginning of civilisation, the black hole, whatever there was *before* the black hole. I would have to check with Stephen Hawking. Physics hurt my brain. I had foolishly elected to study it in my final years of high school, to 'keep my options open', and the only good mark I got was for a poster of the universe, which was basically an art project and had fuck all to do with physics, really.

'You know wha women do?' Don asked me.

'No, what?' I wondered what he was going to say. Have babies? Get their period? Like shoes a lot? There were so many options, the mind boggled.

'They kick you in the *guts*, and then they kick you in the NUTS!' he announced, and I had to bite my lip to stop myself from smiling, and tried to pass it off as a mixture of concerned empathy and intense listening.

'My mates tell me *all the time*, "Don, you're a nice guy!" *And* they tell me that I'm good lookin'! So why carn I fine a woman to cuddlup to at night? Huh? I don't wanna woman to have *sex* with or nothin', I've been there, done that, *believe me*!' He smiled in spite of himself, and I suppressed an involuntary grimace. 'But I just want someone to *hold me* and *touch me*.'

The thought of either of those actions being performed on Don made me feel a bit sick.

'Well, you can't really rush these things,' I said diplomatically, tiptoeing around the screamingly obvious. Maybe he couldn't find someone to *hold him* and *touch him* because he was a misogynist with a drinking problem and a mental health history a mile long. Still, what did I know? Perhaps there was a real catch buried – deeply – underneath all of that stuff. My chaotic boyfriend history spoke for itself, and it said that I had no idea what I was doing, so I was really in no position to judge.

'But I *give up*,' he went on, ignoring me. 'And if I don't havva woman, then I might as well be DEAD . . . *That's* why I wanna kill myself. And *that's* why I drink. Because of the *pain*, in *here*!' He dramatically thumped his chest with a clenched fist.

'I see,' I said, and this is when I must confess to having tuned out a bit. I started thinking about what to have for dinner. Don was so drunk he didn't notice that I wasn't paying attention to him, and even if he had, I was pretty good at looking like I cared when my mind was elsewhere. I wondered if there was any food in my fridge that was still edible, since I hadn't been to the supermarket in a while, or if I should just pick up some sushi on the way home . . . When I dropped back in on Don's monologue, he was still going strong.

'I've made bad choices with women,' Don conceded, 'like that *bitch* I've been seein' lately. She took me for all I was worth . . . At first, it was *great* with us! She fell in love with me at the casino at first sight! She said she didn't care about all-a the money I won, *she wanted me for* ME. Well, she's a *fucken liar*! And you know what she didta me?'

'No.' But she sounded like a bit of a grifter, so my guess was that she drank her weight in Moët, got him to buy her a Louis Vuitton handbag and a pair of Christian Louboutin heels, then disappeared into the night. I pictured her looking like Sharon Stone in *Casino*, and their doomed 'love' affair taking place in Las Vegas. I often went off on imaginative tangents like this, but the truth was always a lot less glamorous.

'After I let her move *all* her *shit* into my place, she went off with a fucken *sugar daddy*! He's 62! And she's 22! It's *disgusting*!' he said, confounded and appalled. Don didn't exactly seem like a spring chicken himself, but the big-drinking, hard-living patients were often quite a lot younger than they looked.

'How old are you, Don?' I asked him, and he hesitated while his pissed brain ever so slowly did the maths.

'Fifty-three,' he said finally, which meant Don *was* actually as old as he looked. So a 32-year age difference was fine, but a 40-year age gap was disgusting. Interesting. Don was a curious individual, and thankfully, finally, he was running out of verbal steam. He picked up his sandwich again, and I looked down at the page of notes I had scribbled while Don was venting. They were pretty threadbare and just said, *0.295*, *slurring* ++, <u>hates</u> women and *guts & nuts*. I couldn't really pass it off as a Drug and Alcohol assessment so I started over and steered Don back to the basics. I had learnt a lot about him and his various gripes, but not much of it was very clinically relevant.

'Okay . . . well, Don, I just need to ask you a few questions, if that's okay . . . Do you have any pain at the moment?'

'Oh yeah, I've got pain, all right,' he said with a pathetic look on his face, like a puppy that had just had its nose rubbed in its own shit. He was so melodramatic I felt like rolling my eyes, but I exercised restraint.

'I've got pain *here*,' he pointed at his heart, 'and *here*,' he said, pointing at his head.

I paused. 'I meant physical pain.'

'What?' he stalled. 'Oh . . . no. But emotional pain, and mental pain . . . I'm in *agony*. You should just *shoot me*,' he said, wallowing in his misery like a sow in a mud bath.

'I would if I could, Don,' I told him, and I meant it, too. I know, I'm a bad person.

'Thanks, love,' he said, 'that means a lot to me.' And his eyes welled up with tears again and I went to get him a box of tissues.

I'm pleased to report that Don's luck with women turned around. The next time I saw him at the hospital, he was accompanying his new girlfriend, Barb, and they both wanted to do something about their drinking. They had met in an Alcoholics Anonymous meeting, then gone to a pub to talk, and in retrospect, it hadn't been the ideal location for a first date. Their two-month 'honeymoon' period was a non-stop cask wine binge that had only drawn to a close when they arrived at Emergency, so they were both steaming, and held hands as they sat in the waiting room. When I called out Barb's name, Don came with her. They were a two-for-one deal, and the combined alcohol vapours were hideously overpowering.

'We need help! We needa detox!' Don announced, and Barb began to cry. 'Babe! Don't you cry, darlin'! It's okay!' Don cradled her face in his hands and Barb broke down, blubbering. 'It's gunna be *fiiine*! I love you *sooo* much, babe! Come on, we're in this together!' And he planted a lingering, wet kiss on her lips.

Oh, good god . . . I averted my eyes and wanted to barf.

I hadn't said a word to either one of them. They were in their own little pissed world, two 50-something alcoholics acting like 15-year-olds and too drunk to curb their soap opera theatrics. One of the Emergency nurses walked by, grinning at my misfortune and how much my job sucked, as I looked away and sighed and waited for them to cut the shit. I kind of wished Don was single and suicidal again.

Things I Do Not Understand

There are a lot of things I don't understand, like all languages other than English, economics, and running long distances because you want to and not because you're being chased, but some of the things I saw in Emergency were truly bewildering. People who hurt themselves on purpose, or stuck things up their arse, urethra or vagina that didn't belong there, confused the shit out of me. I was of the school of thought that if you were *meant* to have a carrot up your arse, you probably would have been born with a carrot up your arse, but conversely, I had no issue with changing my naturally boring hair colour . . .

There was a diagnostic category in the Emergency Department database entitled 'Foreign Body In Rectum', which meant that it happened often enough to warrant its own clickable box. I found that fact, alone, shocking. It was right there alongside 'Nosebleed' and 'Suspected Fracture'. Apparently it was commonplace to present to the Emergency Department and seek to have a 'misplaced' object brought back from the point of no return. And the things that people stuck up their bums were just as wildly diverse as the patients who fronted up for retrieval. It was amazing. You name it, and somewhere, *somehow*, it has been up somebody's arse. My personal favourite was the guy who came in with a long-necked, fat-bottomed *vase* up his arse, which was successfully removed in theatre and made its way back to Emergency, intact, where one of the nurses picked it up, saying, 'Wow! What a beautiful vase!' And then dry retched when she found out where it had been and washed her hands for about three hours straight.

Generally, the patient presented to the front desk looking pale, embarrassed, afraid and pained, and the nurses nobly maintained a professional demeanour while the patient concocted some sort of justification for their predicament. There was often a fairly scant description of the events leading up to the lodgement, because frankly *Tomato sauce bottle inserted in rectum* was all the information anyone needed or wanted. The 'why' of the equation was diplomatically left untouched, which I think was the best tack for all parties involved.

The diagnosis of arse tomfoolery always spread like giggling, immature wildfire through Emergency, and the X-rays were in hot demand, like the guy with a set of Russian dolls up his bum. Each doll was clearly visible on the X-ray: a doll inside a doll, inside a doll, inside a rectum. It was hilarious. Well, it was hilarious for everyone except the patient, who had his curtains pulled shut as he waited to go into theatre and hid his face in the pillow whenever anyone came near him.

More disturbing, though, were the stories about people who had attempted to remove the fruit, vegetable, animal or mineral themselves in order to avoid the acute embarrassment of coming into hospital and divulging that they had 'fallen' onto a rolling pin, or 'sat on' a Granny Smith apple. One man had fashioned a coat hanger into a makeshift hook to remove the zucchini wedged in his arse, and ended up shredding the zucchini *and* the interior of his bowel. He was a third-year medical student. Hopefully he turned out to be a better doctor than he was an amateur. And then there was the man who attempted to remove a *goldfish* from his girlfriend's nether regions with a pair of *scissors* because kitchen tongs were just far too unwieldy . . .

A career in nursing sometimes felt like it could qualify as deliberate self-harm, but the real self-harmers were so tragic they made you want to curl up in the foetal position and stay there for the rest of your life. I was not a big fan of pain, personally, and would go to great lengths to avoid it, like staying with shit boyfriends for far longer than I should have, just to avoid the anguish and misery of a breakup. Not counting said shit boyfriends, my own self-harm was more along the lines of cigarette smoking and drunken carelessness, stupid yet gentler exploits compared with the harsh self-directed violence I witnessed on the periphery of the Emergency Department on any given day.

I could feel myself growing numb and gradually becoming desensitised from constant exposure to a catalogue of horrors. The first time I saw somebody's arms and legs latticed with razor cuts, I felt woozy and sick. Eventually, I was just mildly surprised when someone came in with a mode of self-inflicted injury I hadn't seen before, because you thought, *Okay*, now *I've seen everything*, until you saw something worse. And there was *always* something worse coming along.

My drug and alcohol patients harmed themselves every day, drinking methylated spirits and vanilla essence and injecting crushed up tablets until they lost fingers and toes to amputation, and developed fungal infections in their spines and eyes, but their self-harm revolved around self-medication more than self-flagellation, although the end result was not dissimilar.

If there was a prize for hurting yourself the most, I would have given it to Sylvie, although she had some pretty stiff competition from a few other committed patients. Sylvie had, in no particular order: pulled out all of her toenails, and swallowed 280 nails, 50 (*open*) safety pins, 150 drawing pins, several boxes of razor blades, cutlery, five steak knives and handfuls of tampons that expanded in her gut. Unsurprisingly, she'd had a colostomy to bypass her decimated bowel, which meant having an adhesive bag stuck to her abdomen that literally filled with crap like a dirty balloon, then was thrown away and replaced. Wearing your bowel eliminations in a pouch on the outside of your body, like some grotesque satchel, was awful enough, but Sylvie also had schizophrenia, borderline personality disorder, constant suicidal thoughts, Coke-bottle glasses *and* frizzy hair you couldn't do anything with. She couldn't catch a break.

You could tell something was a bit 'off' with Sylvie, without knowing anything about her history, but she was otherwise quite sweet and polite and didn't complain when there was a long delay to see a doctor. She just sat in the waiting room with her hands folded in her lap, waiting endlessly. The only person Sylvie was a bastard to was Sylvie, and her focus was sadly immovable. The drug and alcohol patients I saw were a piece of cake in comparison. She, and other complex patients of her ilk, seemed unfixable, but the fact that they were presenting to hospital, and were not yet dead, was considered a treatment 'win'. And if *that* was winning, then I would hate to see what losing looked like.

Like Sylvie, Monday was another dedicated perpetrator of self-harm who was a regular in Emergency, en route to the Burns Unit. Things could really only have been worse if her parents had called her Sunday Evening, when even the most cheerful and well-adjusted person is bummed out by the thought of the imminent working week or having to wake up for school.

Monday would pour petrol on herself and set it on fire so her legs and arms sizzled like teppanyaki, or press herself against anything scalding hot, like the exhaust pipe of a motorbike, or an iron, until her skin melted away like butter. She lived on the streets, but had been to the Burns Unit so many times for such prolonged stays that it was her most frequent home away from homelessness. The scar tissue from grafting meant her skin resembled a gruesome patchwork quilt, and she had burns on top of burns because she was rapidly running out of real estate. Whenever I walked through the waiting room to my office and heard Monday asking somebody for a lighter, I was sure her mangled arms and legs on full display in short shorts and a t-shirt made it quite an uneasy request.

It seemed every self-harmer had their own unique take, and the more I learnt, the less appalled I felt, but the person who really got to me was a 55-year-old man called Charles.

He had a stomach wound he could not leave alone, and was forever opening it up and putting things like scissors and sticks in it. One time he managed to perforate his bowel with a plastic knife from the hospital food court, and almost died when faecal matter began oozing into his gut.

My first meeting with Charles took place on a curiously slow afternoon. I had randomly approached him because his beard was stained a brassy orange from smoking and he looked like he might enjoy a drink or 40. He was lying on a trolley, staring off into space, and smiled brightly when I said hello. He was obviously bored out of his brain, so we had that much in common at least.

'What brings you to hospital today, Charles?' I asked, after we had introduced ourselves and shaken hands.

'Oh, this,' he said casually, lifting up his jumper.

There was a biro in his stomach that had been pushed almost all the way in, so I could just see the tip of it poking out. My eyes nearly popped out of my head. I was either going to puke or faint if I stuck around, so I took off rather abruptly, and avoided Charles whenever I saw him in hospital, which was a weekly occurrence on average. It was self-preservation. Charles's guts and I were never going to be good friends.

Anatomy textbooks make everything look neat and colourful and tidy, when people's insides really look like meat trays, organs squished in next to each other, all soft and mushy and bloody. Call me crazy, but I think we have skin for a reason. We're not supposed to create windows in it, and we're *sure as shit* not supposed to prop them open by filling them with stationery and other inanimate objects.

There were two other ladies with self-harming tendencies who also gave me The Fear, and always seemed to be around when I was working. Whenever Lorna's name flashed up on the computer, I was curious to see what she had done this time, because she was always upping the ante. She drank Windex and detergent, swallowed needles and fishhooks, and stuck things in her vagina, like knitting needles, other people's dentures, cigarette butts and rocks.

And then there was Michelle, who took 'cutting' to unheard of new heights – or depths. She cut her arms so often and so deeply that unless she hit *bone*, she felt cheated.

She even had a system: razor blades, an ice-cream bucket, and towels on the floor to catch the overflow, and then she bled into the bucket like a slaughtered animal and called an ambulance before she passed out from blood loss. I read this information and while I could understand the words, I could not fathom the reality.

The last time I saw Michelle, she had appeared like a sad mirage at the counter, with dirty bandages still on her arm from her last presentation days earlier. I was checking something on the computer at the front desk and she thought I was the triage nurse, which was a reasonable assumption.

'I'm depressed,' she said flatly, lifting her shirt to show me a centimetre-deep laceration zigzagging across the entire width of her abdomen. The computer said this was her 254th presentation to the Emergency Department, and the computer system had only been in existence for six years.

Ah, great. Now I was depressed, too.

For a so-called 'caring profession' it felt like I had been given an excellent induction in learning how *not* to care, but you were no use to anyone having an emotional breakdown in the corner. When you saw something really horrible or sad, you freaked out internally for a second, then brushed it aside. That's what we were paid for.

Whenever I met with my non-nurse friends and recounted the bleak litany of gore that constituted my workday, I was reminded how shocking the details were to a civilian. I had already assimilated Michelle's and Sylvie's woe, filing them neatly under 'work stories' in my mind, but like exposure to asbestos, I wondered if there would be any lasting or harmful consequences as a result, and what I had already absorbed via osmosis.

Epilogue

I think it's fair to describe my relationship with nursing as love/hate, and it's not nursing's fault that after 12 months, on average, I begin to hate its guts, no matter where in its myriad houses I reside, or how comfortable, rewarding or enlightening I may find them for a time.

I've come to realise that I have a limited attention span, generally, and especially so when it comes to work. A year is the maximum amount of time I should spend doing *any* job, no matter how great the coffee might be, or how much I love my workmates, and even in the absence of night shift. Regardless of how good I have it, my interest has begun to wane by the first anniversary.

After 12 months in Bone Marrow Transplant I was done, but ended up staying for three years. I took a four-month break to travel overseas and whenever I thought of returning to the Transplant Unit, I experienced an inner hysteria that just wouldn't quit. I couldn't stomach the thought of going back, so I went to Detox instead, and in more ways than one.

The smell of metabolising alcohol being secreted from my patients' skin and witnessing their self-driven demise turned me off drinking for the years I was there. No doubt if I had been partial to heroin or pills it would have had the same curative effect. Alcohol was something of a chicken and egg scenario for me, although I wasn't sure which was the chicken and which was the egg. The sadness of Bone Marrow made me want to drink and the alcoholics in Detox made me *not* want to drink, but the verbal abuse and threats of violence in Detox made me wistful for the Transplant Unit, which made me want to drink . . . I was happier working in Detox, so perhaps the answer is as simple as that. I didn't drink because I didn't feel such an acute need for escapism anymore.

After a year in Detox, seeing the same people coming in with the same patter, the same stories with only minor variations, I realised that, although a lot more patients died in Bone Marrow Transplant, they actually had a better prospect for recovery than the alcoholics who made up 70% of my patient quota every day. *That* was depressing, although it was depressing in a 'You're slowly killing yourself!' way, while Bone Marrow was depressing in an 'Oh, you're dying right *now*' fashion.

A skip to the side to work in Emergency kept me interested in drug and alcohol nursing well past the usual 12-month tenure. My time in Emergency gave me an education in what *not* to do, more than anything, but as always, I began to care less and less and it was eventually time to move on. I left the cocoon of the hospital this time, and literally entered another world: the community methadone clinic. *Oh*, the stories I could tell! But it's very unlikely I would be thanked for it. Mostly it was bleak, although I did laugh when one of the patients asked for a copy of her urine drug test results to take to her dealer as proof that he was ripping her off: 'See this? There's *NO HEROIN* in it!' It would have been funnier still if she didn't have five young children at home.

Lest I have painted a miserable or misleading picture, nursing has been very good to me and, after seven years, I think I'm *finally* getting the hang of it; perhaps not the most reassuring news for the patients I've previously looked after to hear. Nursing and I were an arranged marriage, of sorts. Neither one of us was the other's first choice or dream come true, but we've grown comfortable in each other's company and, while it may not be passionate love, there is a bond that will more than likely last for life.

It would be remiss of me not to point out all the gifts that nursing has provided me with: many totally excellent friends; escape from the deadbeat employment routine; a job title I'm not embarrassed to admit to; money to travel; shift flexibility that enabled me to go out drinking several nights a week; sobriety (for a time); and a glimpse into the unpleasant future that awaited me as a smoker if I continued to partake. It has introduced me to people I would probably never have met otherwise and I suspect I am a better person for having known them, and it has made me feel that what I do for a living is worth doing most of the time. Finally, it has given me something to say, although

Get Well Soon!

I've been thinking lately that a little time apart might be healthy. Like a failing love affair, some time out could help me grow nostalgic and rediscover the depth of my feelings because there have been times when I truly loved my job. Right now, though, my soul feels tired and I'm more restless than usual. And as circumstance would have it, after seven years of employment I have accumulated long service leave, and this book, and I hear New York City is lovely in autumn . . .

It's not you, Nursing, it's me.

Acknowledgements

Thank you kindly indeed, Alexandra Payne, for everything writing-related and for being altogether awesome. Many thanks also to Kylie Mason and everyone at University of Queensland Press.

For all the love, moral support and hot meals, I thank Ciara Moss, and the Chambers, Rodrigues and Walkley families.

Big love to Benjamin, Dan Ian, K-Schulz, Rachell, Sean, Seja and Vickysan for being so kind, supportive and attractive.

And thank you to *all* my friends in nursing, and the patients who, for better or worse, made my days at work memorable.